Asia and Japan

The search for modernization and identity

ASIA AND JAPAN

The search for modernization and identity

Edited by Andrew J L Armour

With a Foreword by
Dr Derek Brewer and Sir John Butterfield

Keio University, Tokyo

The Athlone Press
London and Dover, New Hampshire

First published in Great Britain in 1985
by The Athlone Press
44 Bedford Row, London WC1R 4LY
and 51 Washington Street, Dover, NH 03820

Copyright © 1985 Keio University

British Library Cataloguing in Publication Data
Asia and Japan: the search for modernization
    and identity.
    1.   East Asia–Economic conditions   2.   Asia,
    Southeastern–Economic conditions
    I.   Armour, Andrew J.L.
    330.95'0428   HC460.5

    ISBN 0–485–11261–2

Library of Congress Cataloging-in-Publication Data
Asia and Japan
    Originally presented as papers at the Keio International Sym-
posium on 'Asia and Japan', Tokyo, Nov. 7–11, 1983, sponsored by
Keio University.
    Includes index.
    Contents: Introduction — Asia and Japan / Ishikawa Tadao —
Towards a new age of prosperity in the Asia–Pacific region / Park
Choong Hoon — [etc.]
    1. Japan—Economic conditions—1868- —Congresses. 2. Asia,
Southeastern—Economic conditions—Congresses. 3. China—Eco-
nomic conditions— 1949- —Congresses. 4. Japan—Relations—
Asia —Congresses. 5. Asia—Relations—Japan —Congresses. I.
Armour, Andrew J. L., 1954- . II. Keio International Symposium
on 'Asia and Japan' (1983: Tokyo, Japan) III. Keio Gijuku Daigaku.
HC462.7.A83 1985   337.5052   85–9029
ISBN 0–485–11261–2

Typesetting by TJB Photosetting Ltd, South Witham, Lincolnshire
Printed and bound in Great Britain by
Biddles Ltd, Guildford and King's Lynn

Foreword

As British academics, we are proud to be associated with Keio University, one of Japan's oldest universities, and take great pleasure in introducing these papers from the Keio International Symposium of 1983 to a wide Western public.

A glance at the list of contributors and their titles shows that this is a remarkable collection of papers from many different international and intellectual points of view. Everyone recognizes that Japan has become a major world economic force but this book shows how seriously the Japanese are now facing the need for a further stage of ethical and cultural advance alongside their great economic development. There was no question of a concealed or indirect cultural imperialism at the Symposium; on the contrary, it was distinguished by frank self-criticism. This is detectable from the distinguished first paper by Ishikawa Tadao, President of Keio University, and is discernible throughout in the remarkably generous acceptance of criticism coming from non-Japanese contributors. Such an underlying attitude witnesses the admirable confidence and willingness to accept responsibility, with a corresponding concern for the future, which mark Japanese culture just when the rest of us seem to be losing our way.

The central question is precisely that of confidence in one's sense of cultural identity. The Japanese have been remarkable for the way that, even after heavy military defeat, they have lost neither their own culture nor their sense of national identity and direction.

Even after a century of deliberate and diligent westernization they have not cut themselves from their roots but have retained their traditions. Now the task is seen to be to develop beyond recovery and consolidation, and to create a forward-looking national identity for Japan extending into the twenty-first century, incorporating the good but leaving out the bad of Western industrial culture. By so doing, Japan may offer the world a new humane model of individual, national and international self-realization and co-operation. We must hope that a new model can be created which will transcend the conflicts between East and West, North and South, past and present, industrialization and conservation. Japan, and Asia in general, are stirring to take such a new initiative. The virtues of solidarity, hard work and rationality which have brought about Japan's tremendous achievements are not merely economic factors in themselves: once such energies and virtues are turned towards the questions of living together in an increasingly crowded world, they will surely provide us with answers that could benefit the whole of the human race.

So we are delighted to commend this valuable book. It provokes the Western reader to think more about possible new worlds.

DEREK BREWER, Litt D, Ph D
Honorary Member of the Japan Academy
Hon. LL D, Keio University
Master of Emmanuel College, Cambridge

Sir JOHN BUTTERFIELD, Kt, OBE, MD, FRCP
Hon. D Med Sci, Keio University
Master of Downing College, Cambridge
Vice-Chancellor, University of Cambridge

Cambridge, December 1984

Preface

The ten essays included in this volume are derived from papers presented at the Keio International Symposium on 'Asia and Japan', held in Tokyo from 7 to 11 November 1983. After the official opening, the keynote address on 'Asia and Japan' was made by Professor Ishikawa Tadao, President of Keio University. Over the following three days, papers were read by the guest speakers: distinguished politicians, academics and intellectuals, representing nine different areas of the Asia-Pacific region. On the final day, an extended panel discussion was held on the theme 'Asia and Japan – Identity and Diversity', a brief summary of which is included in the Introduction to this volume.

The order in which these essays appear is the same as that in which the symposium papers were read. Some were originally presented in English, while others have been translated; it should be borne in mind that later editing may have resulted in minor differences between these essays and the original papers. Contributors' names are given in the order customarily used in the person's country of origin, and the use of honorifics has been kept to a minimum.

As regards romanization, the Hepburn system is employed for Japanese words and names, though omitting macrons on well-known place-names or words that have entered the English language. The *pinyin* system, adopted in 1979 as the official transcription method in China, is used for Chinese. In certain cases – such as Chiang Kai-shek and Yangtze Kiang – the more familiar Wade-Giles romanizations are also provided. Diacritical marks have been omitted, although in the case of Dr Huang's paper Chinese characters have been supplied in the form of a glossary.

Acknowledgments

This book is the end product of a long process that can be traced back to the initial planning and preparation for the 2nd Keio International Symposium, and there are naturally many people who have contributed to it, in one way or another. Unfortunately, it is not possible to mention everyone by name, but special thanks are due to the translators of those papers originally drafted in Japanese and Chinese: Charles Quinn for Professor Suzuki's paper; Shi Lihe, Kin Bunkyō, and Matsukawa Yūko for Professor Sun's paper. The keynote address given by Professor Ishikawa was translated by myself in consultation with Dr Sugiura Noriyuki. I would also like to thank all my colleagues on the Editorial Committee for their support, especially the Chairman, Professor Matsubara Hideichi. And finally, I should like to express my gratitude to Professor Takamiya Toshiyuki and Kin Bunkyō for the tireless guidance and valuable suggestions which they provided during the editing stages.

Keio University, Tokyo   ANDREW J.L. ARMOUR

Introduction

In 1858, Fukuzawa Yukichi (1835–1901) established an institute of higher education called Keio Gijuku; this is now known as Keio University, one of Japan's most prestigious private universities. Fukuzawa was the first Japanese to introduce Western civilization to Japan on this formal level and was a pioneer in the so-called *Bunmei Kaika*, or civilization and enlightenment movement. Having travelled to both Europe and the United States, he received the impression that Asia was still semi-civilized in comparison with the West and was therefore in need of enlightenment. Thenceforth, he devoted himself to the development and modernization of Japan, and he is without doubt partly responsible for the country's present high position in the family of nations. It is no coincidence that his portrait now decorates the Japanese banknote of highest denomination.

Among the many monuments to Fukuzawa that still remain, perhaps Keio, with its famous *Enzetsukan* (Hall of Public Speaking), is the most conspicuous, standing serene on Mita hill and surrounded by the hyperactive metropolis of Tokyo. With its tradition of enlightenment and internationalism, it is only natural that Keio should play host to an international symposium. The first of these was held in 1979. Entitled 'Dimensions of Global Interdependence — Harmony and Conflict in the Contemporary World', it was designed to focus on the concept of a 'global society', a reflection of the increasing level of global interdependence and the finite nature of the world's ecosystem. In November 1983, as one of the events held to commemorate Keio's 125th anniversary, the 2nd International Symposium was opened on the theme 'Asia and Japan'.

Whereas the first Symposium was intended as an introduction, the second, in effect, forms 'Chapter One' of a continuing quest. The focus is on Japan and its Asian neighbours, countries which boast old traditions and a rich cultural heritage. For these nations, the unavoidable meeting with the West that occurred in the nineteenth century was an experience so traumatic that it threw many of them into turmoil. There was military aggression, imperialism and colonialism, perhaps on a scale never before experienced, but none of this was new. What really shocked the Asians, as Ishikawa Tadao explains in his keynote address, was the view that they received of themselves. In addition to their obviously superior technology, the Westerners brought with them a world view that saw Asia as a stagnant backwater in the current of history. The shock of this revelation created an acute awareness of crisis; the Asians felt that they had taken a wrong turning somewhere in the past. It was time to change direction, discard tradition and modernize – to 'westernize'.

Westernization can certainly bring many material benefits; nobody in Asia has been more enthusiastic about it than the Japanese, and as a result their country has become very prosperous. However, there are also drawbacks. While avidly absorbing Western ideas and precepts, the Japanese have become intellectually estranged from the rest of Asia. Despite being indebted to Asia in many ways – for natural resources, energy, trade and security – Japan's perception of, and attitudes towards, its neighbours are often Western-oriented. Given its economic power, it cannot help but exert a powerful influence on the region, but unless it can rediscover its Asian identity, misunderstandings are sure to occur. Not only is this unfortunate, but it may even endanger the continued development of an area which at times has to cope with serious regional conflicts, civil unrest, natural and industrial disasters, and mounting debts, all set against the backdrop of superpower rivalry. Old enemies have joined hands, but while the remnants of nineteenth-century colonialism disappear, security concerns demand increasing attention. And stability is a necessary condition for continued modernization.

Westernization is a process that has affected Asia in so many ways and to such an extent that it is beyond the scope of any one book to deal with it comprehensively. However, the papers presented at the 2nd International Symposium provide a montage of views that build into a fascinating picture of a complex phenomenon. Some contributors chose to look back to the last century in order to examine the roots of the process; others discuss the problems and challenges of the present, or even peer into the next century, to the development that lies beyond mere 'westernization'.

First, Ishikawa Tadao discusses Fukuzawa's programme based on de-orientalization, using this as a springboard for a philosophical reflection on the historical significance of modernization in Asia, especially in Japan during the Meiji era (1868–1912). Parallel to the industrialization one finds on the physical plane, he describes the search for a new identity that occurs on the spiritual plane. His conclusions point to a future path of development that is neither Western nor Oriental: a fusion of horizons.

Treating the same era is Sommai Hoontrakool, who focuses on the political rather than the philosophical. In comparing the reigns of King Chulalongkorn of Thailand and Emperor Meiji of Japan, he seeks the basic reasons why similar modernization programmes produced different results in two countries which shared several characteristics. It would seem that Japan had made quiet progress in many fields during the isolated centuries of the Tokugawa period (1600–1868), something which gave her a head-start.

The devastating impact of the West on the artistic life of a people is vividly described by Albert Wendt. Although not strictly speaking 'Asian' – an appellation which is in any case notoriously difficult to define – the Pacific region is a close neighbour and provides invaluable material for a study of the decolonization process. His views provide us with a fresh insight into recent developments in such places as New Caledonia, as well as into the mind of the new, post-colonial artist.

Modernization must depend to a great extent on education, and this is the theme of Rayson Lisung Huang's paper on the university as an agent of change. Special reference is made to the contribution of Japanese institutions, like Keio, to the development of China in the late nineteenth and early twentieth centuries. But he warns that universities can only play such a catalytic role if they are granted sufficient autonomy.

Sun Shangqing addresses the future of China, particularly with regard to energy and technology – the keys to sustained growth. Another key to successful development is co-operation with the other major power in the region, Japan. If, as is often suggested, the Asia–Pacific region becomes the growth-pole of the twenty-first century, then these two nations will un-doubtedly become the giants of the future.

This idea of future prosperity for the region is taken up by Park Choong Hoon, who urges Japan to take the initiative in rediscovering an Asia–Pacific identity. By making use of the neglected cultural heritage and powerful potential of Asia, and by avoiding over-dependence on the West, new horizons will open up. An important part of this process must be 'agreed specialization' as a means to improve regional co-operation and co-ordination. The natural resource which he stresses is the young generation.

Mochtar Lubis asks whether Japan has the ability once again to become an inspiration for Asia, as it was after the 1905 defeat of Russia. He sees a great deal of inequality in the present economic order, something created by First World countries for their own benefit. But with its unique cultural values, Japan is in a position to help reverse the trend and allow the Third World to share in some of the fruits of modernization.

This can only come about, however, if attitudes change. Japan's unhappy tradition of ignoring its neighbours is examined by Suzuki Takao, who suggests rejecting the West-ern idol since it has outlived its usefulness. Despite being the region's largest economic power, Japan has inevitable blind spots; by refocusing its attention on Asia, Japan may indeed help to contribute to a better world.

Escolastica Bince traces the process by which the Philippines developed a modern financial system with a Central Bank that helps to stimulate further development. Many useful conclu-sions can be drawn from the author's description of the role of banking in a developing Asian country.

Finally, the importance of maintaining stability, even at the expense of economic growth, is stressed by Mahathir bin Mohamad. Attention is drawn to the peculiar problems faced by a multiracial Asian country in which modernization must be seen in context as just one of a number of important goals for a developing nation.

After delivering their papers at the Symposium, the guest

speakers and the President of the University participated in a panel discussion on the theme 'Asia and Japan – Identity and Diversity'. Among the topics discussed was the problem of actually defining development, for unless the qualitative content is emphasized, development will itself create fresh economic inequalities. Lessons must be learned from the past, and industrialization has to be assessed for its impact on society. Industrialization causes an acceleration in the change experienced by a nation, and this in turns leads to global standardization, which reduces diversity and may even annihilate a culture. The loss of tradition gives rise to instability and people begin to question the actual purpose of modernization. But these changes are as inevitable as they are irreversible, and perhaps the surest way to shift the course of history in a favourable direction is to foster increased co-operation and a sense of community among the many countries in the region. Only then can there be a dawning of 'Asia's century'.

Asia and Japan

Introduction: development and de-orientalization

Established by Fukuzawa Yukichi in 1858 during a period of considerable political and social turmoil, Keio Gijuku later came to play a significant role in the modernization of Japan. Modernization has been achieved, but Fukuzawa's ideals and achievements are, if anything, even more important today than they were a century ago. Consequently, a historical reappraisal of them is a fitting way to mark this 125th anniversary. Such a reappraisal is extremely relevant, not only for Keio University and those connected with it, but also for a great many people, working in diverse fields, who are today confronted with a variety of complex issues.

When one comes to consider Fukuzawa's ideals and how they have been handed down during the last century or so, it becomes clear that a discussion of the relationship between Asia and Japan's modernization is essential. The reason for this is that his ideals were founded on an acute awareness of two historical aspects of the period in which he lived. The first of these was the feudal stratification of contemporary Japanese society. The second was the fact that Japan was a part of Asia, a region which was being tossed about in a tempest; this was, of course, the result of the colonial expansionism by the Western powers.

Fukuzawa responded by setting forth a programme for social change; this was the necessary condition for the realization of his ideals. Keio Gijuku, the *Jiji-Shimpō* newspaper, and this Hall of Public Speaking are impressive achievements, but they form only a small part of this considerable programme developed by Fukuzawa. What he was aiming at, and what the programme was designed to create, was a democratic society in which it was justice that counted, not class or power. Essential tools in the realization of this goal were two freedoms: freedom

6

of speech and freedom of education. We can be certain that, beyond this, lay the greater goal of creating a country that was truly independent and which could make its own contribution to the world from which it had for so long been cut off. In order to achieve these goals, it is clear that Fukuzawa saw the necessity for reforming society *in toto* – what we now refer to as 'modernization'.

Fukuzawa Yukichi is renowned for his unusually profound knowledge concerning foreign matters; at the time, few Japanese knew anything about the world outside. However, it should be stressed that more important than this was his deep understanding of the basic nature of the world and the tide of the times. As you are no doubt aware, he developed his modernization programme based on this understanding and centred around the concept of *datsua-ron*, which I will translate as 'de-orientalization'. What this involved was the metaphysical detachment of the country from the entity known as Asia. In fact, Fukuzawa was switching from the temporal dimension of social change to the spatial dimension in which Japan would 'migrate' from East to West. In this way he lent immediacy and realism to his programme, at the same time as impressing people with the urgency and importance of the issues which faced them.

De-orientalization thus became the fundamental political agenda for modern Japan; it provided the logic and the rhetoric for the process by which to change society. In other words, it served as a source of inspiration for the self-definition and actions of Fukuzawa and many of his contemporaries. It is totally meaningless, therefore, to discuss de-orientalization out of the context of the larger process of development. What is important to understand is that de-orientalization was not just the process of leaving Asia and joining the West – in other words, 'westernization' – and through westernization achieving the final goal of modernization. It would be more accurate to say that de-orientalization was a political and cultural expression of the concept of development, a concept which envisaged a later estrangement from the West and subsequent establishment of an independent nation, as well as the restoration of the dignity of its citizens.

Through the process of modernization Japan has, of course,

succeeded in becoming a member of the international community of industrialized nations. At the same time, it has also strengthened its ties with the other countries and peoples of Asia. If one looks back over the history of Japan's relations with Asia, it becomes apparent that they are an extremely complex tangle of two distinct threads: confrontation and co-operation. There still exist, of course, unhappy memories of a time when these relations were at their lowest ebb. However, at the core of this relationship as it has developed over the last century – including all its military and diplomatic aspects, economic development and technical co-operation projects, and cultural exchanges – can be found the concepts of development and de-orientalization which were propounded by Fukuzawa Yukichi so long ago. I do not believe that we can hope for a mutually prosperous relationship in the future without giving proper consideration to his philosophy. Today, more than ever, the achievement of national independence and dignity is a pressing concern for many countries. Herein lies the significance of the basic theme 'Asia and Japan', the theme chosen for this Symposium.

In contributing to the discussion on Asia and Japan I shall concentrate on one of the major issues: the historical significance of the modernization of Asia over the last century or so. For this I have chosen a philosophical reflection on Japan's experience of modernization. It is my earnest hope that this will point the way to the future of Asia and Japan.

Rude awakening

What is Asia? This is an extremely difficult question to answer. Whenever we try to reflect upon what is really meant by 'Asia', we are forced to accept that there is no all-encompassing definition available. Of course, there are numerous – though tentative – definitions of Asia, each formulated to satisfy a specific, limited purpose. Perhaps the most obvious that come to mind are geographical and cultural definitions, but neither of these will adequately serve our purpose here. In the context of a discussion on modernization, 'Asia' becomes highly elusive, defying definition. And the reason for this is that the 'Asia' which we are considering is not a spatial concept, but an articulation of historical consciousness.

To risk stating the obvious, I should like to stress that, since we ourselves are Asians, any definition of Asia by us is necessarily an act of self-definition. The East has its own view of Asia; the West has another. In a straightforward model, one might hope to synthesize an all-embracing definition from the juxtaposition of two such disparate views: that of the insider and that of the outsider. However, in this case, a mere juxtaposition is inadequate, and even misleading.

In order to obtain a real understanding of the dynamic process of historical change involved in modernization, and of the awareness of crisis that stimulated Asians to embark on such a hazardous undertaking, it is necessary to comprehend the nature of their self-definition. Instead of there being two parallel views of Asia – one from within, and one from without – the two became intertwined with each other, thus affording Asians a view from both perspectives simultaneously.

Before describing how and why such a situation came about, I should like to emphasize that the Asian people most certainly possessed their own historical consciousness, and one which was extremely old. Famous historians, such as Si-ma Qian and Ibn Khaldun, immediately come to mind; but, without having to present any evidence, I can say it is widely accepted that the Asians possessed a highly original, systematic concept of both the world and history, a concept which has been transmitted down through the centuries, nurtured within each of the traditional cultures of Asia. It is also a fact that these Asian cultures, through a process of interaction and fusion which has been repeated throughout their history, have generated and transformed their own unique, historical consciousness.

Why was it, then, that the Asians – despite having this venerable historical consciousness, together with centuries of accumulated tradition – suddenly decided to change course, to search for a new definition of Asia? I have already mentioned that it was an awareness of crisis that induced them to make this drastic decision; but what was it that gave rise to such an awareness?

The contacts which Asia had with the West were substantially different from those it had had with other civilizations.

One reason for this difference lies in the West's all-embracing world view, backed up with a hitherto undreamt-of technological system, complete with the social structure and ideology needed to support it. But perhaps more important has been the fact that the West's compellingly powerful world view, and especially its dazzling techno-scientific system, has seemed to Asian eyes to possess universality.

The meeting which occurred between modern Asia and the West was not merely a 'contact' with a foreign culture. We cannot underestimate the impact which it had and the fact that it was interpreted by the Asians as an encounter with something both superior and universal. From that point on, Asia's self-definition came to be determined according to standards which were external, and apparently universal. The old, internal self-definition was abandoned. The evolutionary theory of civilization, implying as it did the stage-theory of development, was the direct offspring of this new world view, a world view that assumed – explicitly or otherwise – that the West was the touchstone by which the rest of the world should be measured.

Once the West took on this aspect of a superior entity boasting universality, it immediately changed from being an outsider to being an observer, and one which saw things objectively. Naturally, applying its own standards, the West saw Asia as a civilization that was backward, slumbering and stagnant. This was to be expected. However, because of its perceived universality, this Western definition of Asia came to exert a powerful influence on the Asians' view of themselves.

In effect, the 'eyes' of the West became absorbed and internalized within the Asians' own perspective. It was as if they were able to see themselves reflected in a mirror, a mirror which was entirely objective and unbiased. It is one thing to be aware of another's viewpoint or opinion, but quite another to accept it as the objective truth. This is what generated the awareness of crisis experienced by Asians in the last century. The dual perspective – from both inside and out – is what provided the basic conceptual framework for the move towards self-change, towards modernization. And it was the feeling of crisis which provided the stimulus, the inner dynamism that fuelled self-change.

However, all forms of self-change contain, to some extent, a measure of self-criticism, and even self-destruction. Entailing the risk of severe trauma, modernization was thus a path fraught with hazards, whose consequences extended much farther than had been envisaged.

Passage through fire

The Western countries, which had experienced the Industrial Revolution, possessed overwhelming power. Confronted by this, and recognizing that the foreigners' advanced technological system was something universal, Asia concluded that the adoption of such a system was unavoidable. It was therefore obliged to adopt as models the social system and ideology that had produced and supported the technological system. Asia determined that its own past and present were 'backward', and that they should therefore be abandoned.

Asia's acceptance of the universality of what it saw had two consequences.

First, without even considering whether or not it might be possible, Asia saw as inevitable the adoption of the social system and world view that had nurtured the technological system of the West. It was inevitable because these things possessed universality. With this awareness, Asia set out enthusiastically on the path of industrialization.

The second consequence concerned not technology, but thought. The West, which had been chosen as a model, possessed a unique, scientific world view. As long as industrialization remained a process that engendered social change, Asia's traditional world view would be challenged by this Western world view. At times, it would even be forced to submit to it. What this meant was the setting out on another, metaphysical path, parallel to the physical path of industrialization. This was a quest for a new spiritual balance involving Asia's outlook on the Universe and Man. The old, traditional equilibrium was upset and a new one was required to replace it. There were many instances where, without succeeding in finding a new balance, the old was quickly abandoned, thus leading to the total disintegration of self-identity. The stronger the tradition to be negated, the more pronounced was the tendency for this collapse of identity to lead to suffering, anxiety, and even remorse.

There was, however, a way out of this dilemma, or at least a fiction which provided temporary relief from the tempest of industrialization and the quest for a new self. In effect, this was a compromise which sought to separate the material world from the spiritual world. The hope was that modernization might entail industrialization, but not necessarily westernization. If this was so, there was surely a possibility of stopping the steady advance of westernization, just as it threatened to finally engulf what remained of the crumbling self. In Japan, this severing of the spiritual world from the material one found expression in the slogan *wakon yōsai*, or 'Japanese spirit, Western learning'. Employing this concept, the Japanese people found temporary relief in the belief that they existed in two different worlds simultaneously, worlds which coexisted without interfering with each other.

This attitude may have been sufficient for some of the population, but for those members of the intellectual elite who were forced to deal directly with the Westerners it was the source of severe tension. This tension arose because they were in the position of faithfully promoting the so-called 'enlightenment' of their society, a role that made them acutely aware of the fact that any attempt to separate the material and spiritual worlds would render impossible the restoration of a national identity.

Industrialization, the physical aspect of modernization, demanded ever more 'enlightenment'. As enlightenment helped to promote industrialization, so the subtle balance between the material and the spiritual was gradually corroded away. This was inevitable. But as this fissure in the metaphysical environment began to widen, there began to erupt pockets of selfish materialism, and – in reaction – various forms of fanatical spiritualism. In the absence of the unifying influence of self-control, the ego sprang to the fore and commenced to destroy at high speed the traditional social systems that had bound society together. Of course, there was also a positive side: as industrialization progressed, the nation prospered, and the quality of life improved. At the same time, various new democratic processes were introduced and these began to function.

Nevertheless, unable to find a new identity which could exert control over the ego, society was forced into a position that made it highly vulnerable to latent fanaticism. Just as the growth of a person's character requires a development of the ego which entails a certain instability, so too must society pay the price of destabilization in order to undergo modernization.

In the case of the individual, egotism and egocentricity may result in anti-social behaviour: ignoring or despising the existence and personal dignity of one's fellow beings. In much the same way, social egocentricity and racial ethnocentricity may lead to arrogance and self-conceit. These appear in the form of aggressive expansionism, anti-foreign chauvinism, ultra-nationalism and fanatical racism.

With the destruction of identity, society lays itself open to great danger, as long as there is no new self to replace the old. The unconfined ego may well be exposed and, making use of the opportunity, begin to strut arrogantly upon the stage. Warfare and other forms of political violence, the destruction of nature, dire poverty amid conspicuous luxury, moral corruption and the paralysis of aesthetic sensibility – surely these are all diseases which beset a society in which the unfettered ego has been allowed to become bloated in the absence of any self-control.

It would appear, however, that most of the major technical problems concerning the modernization of Asia have been resolved. We are now firmly set on the path that leads to the establishment of a new identity, one that is based on mutual understanding.

In the meantime, Western attitudes concerning modernization are changing. From the turn of the century, there has appeared inside the West sharp criticism and doubt concerning the values which were perceived as being universal. People are questioning the absolute universality which was taken for granted. In other words, we are witnessing the birth of an awareness that the scientific world view is, in fact, a very peculiar phenomenon, even within the context of Western history.

Even more important, perhaps, is a discovery that has been made in the East. The various countries of Asia have gone through the traumatic experience of industrialization, working continually to adopt a technological system that is supposed to be universal. However, it has become clear that the process of industrialization is in no way uniform; it is moulded by each country and culture. In fact, one might say that it is the end result of an adaptation to the unique traditions and systems that exist in each Asian country.

People have become aware that development through industrialization is really a development of the self. They are awakening to the fact that modernization is really a movement for both social change and self-change. In each region, each country, and each culture, it takes on a different and unique character. In other words, modernization is relative.

I would postulate, therefore, that modernization is not something to be measured by the yardstick of 'universality'. It is, in effect, the self-realization of each country and culture. Because of this diversity, it naturally leads to a recognition of the existence and dignity of others, and thus to peaceful coexistence. The current growth in international interdependence – both within and without Asia – makes this all the more meaningful and important.

Modernization is neither the abandoning of the East and joining with the West, nor the opposite, the abandoning of the West and returning to the East. In fact, neither of these two options is presently open to Asia. If one were to examine a category such as 'universality', for instance, it would soon become clear to how large an extent our mentality and sensibility as Asians have been influenced by Western culture and thought. However, when Asians employ a cultural category that originated in the West, there is an element of doubt concerning whether it is exactly the same category as that used in the context of the West. I would suggest that they are probably not identical. Nevertheless, this does not infer that Asia is compelled to remain within the bounds of its cultural framework. On the contrary, I would say that, in both Asia and Europe, a new horizon is appearing which will serve as a doorway to a global culture of the future.

In Asia, this horizon is already visible. It represents neither westernization nor orientalization; rather, it is a third path which combines the two.

This inter-fusion of cultural horizons in fact occurs on three different planes. First, there is a fusion between East and West.

Next, there is a fusion between past and future. And finally, there is a reconciliation between material prosperity and spiritual dignity.

When viewed from the perspective of human history, the peoples of both East and West are all insiders; they cannot help being participants. In fact, this is what makes possible the fusion of horizons. And I feel sure that through this horizon-fusing process Asia will eventually be in a position to make a substantial contribution to global culture.

This, I believe, is today's meaning of the 'independence and self-respect' advocated over a century ago by Fukuzawa Yukichi, the founder of our university and champion of development and de-orientalization.

Towards a new age of prosperity in the Asia-Pacific region

PARK CHOONG HOON

It is particularly significant and timely that Keio University, which played an important role in the course of modernization in the latter part of the nineteenth century, has undertaken the initiative of sponsoring a symposium on 'Asia and Japan'.

In fact, with the beginning of the Meiji era, Japan's utmost national goal was to achieve modernization modelled on Western civilization. The success of modernization in the West, and subsequently in Japan, was a tremendous human victory and set the tone for global economic growth. But it is also true that the Japanese have been challenged by constraints on economic growth and, more importantly, by the loss of humanity and values.

Nevertheless, Japan is not the only country faced with the urgent need to seek a new direction for economic and social development. Most nations in the Asia–Pacific region which have pursued Western-oriented development have also begun to feel some limits on further progress, even though the nature and the degree of these limits may be quite different from those in Japan. In this sense, the tasks confronting the nations of the Asia–Pacific region are, I believe, twofold. One is to find ways to achieve economic growth by avoiding over-dependence on the West. The other is to put added emphasis on our traditional values and philosophies, and to learn how to promote and cultivate the spirit of mutual co-operation among the nations of this region, which has been sadly lacking in the co-ordinated pursuit of peace and prosperity.

It is true that the region is composed of nations extremely proud of their own long history, tradition and cultural heritage. They also possess great potential for economic and social development. These factors would certainly permit them, by

16

means of closer co-operation, to realize proper and sustained development.

As many recent reports suggest, it is quite probable that the Asia-Pacific region will become the growth-pole of world development in the twenty-first century, if it succeeds in redefining its proper role. However, despite the fact that we are neighbours, we – the Asia–Pacific nations – do not know and understand each other well enough to capitalize on what we share in common. For example, many intellectuals in Korea feel that Japan is a very remote neighbour.

In this respect, I believe that the main theme of this Symposium is to turn our attention once more to the Asia–Pacific region, and to redefine what tasks we have to carry out in order to achieve common prosperity in the new era.

The need to place Asia's cultural and spiritual heritage in a balanced perspective

First of all, we should admit that the nations of the Asia–Pacific region as a whole have developed their economies mainly by emulating Western models, while often carelessly neglecting our own cultural and spiritual heritages. One of the tasks lying before us, therefore, is to reappraise the merits of Asian traditional values and cultures, and to place them in a proper and balanced perspective so as to provide new, durable foundations for future economic and social development. In other words, it is necessary 'to rediscover an Asia–Pacific identity', and this does not merely mean we should embellish all that is ours in an attitude of unconditional chauvinism. Rather, this effort should aim at exploiting positively the merits of our own spiritual heritages, and at putting them to practical use in order to further economic and social development.

In fact, we cannot deny that Western civilization – based as it is principally on efficiency and materialism – and its consequent economic ethics have greatly contributed not only to modernization, but also to elevating national income and living standards in this region. However, it is also true that Western civilization has sometimes had a negative influence by causing disturbances in traditional values which have often made intellectuals sceptical about future development. By observing international economic development since the early 1970s, we should be able to find cures – both theoretical and practical – for this prolonged recession, and thus enter into a new, prosperous era. The long economic stagnation which we have experienced is not attributable, I believe, only to the temporary disruption in the early 1970s which resulted from factors such as the oil crisis and inflationary recession. In addition to these factors, it is related to the uncertainties caused by the imbalances and mismatches which have been structurally accumulating in the course of managing market economies since the 1950s. That is the reason why, without first implementing positive adjustment policies, we cannot easily expect a healthy economic recovery.

From this point of view, I believe that, for our future prosperity, we should not only enjoy the advantages of Western civilization, Western thought and Western values, but also stress suitable oriental philosophies and ethics. All social phenomena are interconnected and influenced by each other; a disturbance in one sector cannot be rectified without help from the others. For instance, to overcome the economic difficulties which face nearly all the nations of the world, it is important to make use not only of the rationalism founded on Western economic principles, but also of the wisdom taught by oriental philosophies.

Turning to international politics, on the other hand, we are faced with the phenomenon of a continuing polarization of the superpowers. This results in the growing importance of military expenditure among the major nations, thus aggravating the uncertainties which lead to war. On this occasion, I should like to remind you of the human tragedy which can be caused by war games and stress the importance of common efforts for maintaining peace in the Asia–Pacific region, which is an absolute precondition for the realization of economic prosperity. Needless to say, security in this region depends mainly on the strategic policies of the superpowers. However, with the conscious efforts of the nations concerned, the possibility of the outbreak of war can be minimized; in this regard, I should like to appeal to the original peace-loving nature of the people of the Asia–Pacific region.

The government of the Republic of Korea, for instance, has on many occasions proposed the unconditional opening of bilateral talks with the regime of North Korea. These proposals should be understood as an expression of our firm intention to reach agreement between the two parties directly concerned; this must precede all other efforts to recover peace on the Korean peninsula.

Through my service in government during the rapid economic growth of the 1960s and 1970s, I have become firmly convinced that economic growth can be realized, provided there is political and social stability. It must be the same with the other nations in the Asia–Pacific region. What we need, therefore, are concerted actions for the maintenance of peace and stability, necessary conditions for ensuring the prosperity of the next generation.

The Asia–Pacific region as a source of new dynamism for future world economic development

The need for a reappraisal of the Asia–Pacific region derives also from its great economic potential, as seen in its factor endowments and its development dynamism. Many scholars have forecast the dawning of a new era in the twenty-first century which will be characterized by the emergence of this region as a leading economic power. And, as most reports agree, it is certain to emerge as a new growth-pole of the world economy.

The Asia–Pacific region includes five advanced countries – the United States, Japan, Canada, Australia, and New Zealand – the newly industrializing countries of East Asia, and the ASEAN nations. It constitutes the world's largest market, with nearly seven hundred million people in 1980 – three times the size of the EEC. The region also outranks the EEC in terms of income, accounting for about 40 per cent of the world's GNP, and it is endowed with abundant resources, which constitute a major advantage over other regions. It accounts for about 30 per cent of world energy production, and 40 per cent of energy consumption. Moreover, abundant forests and rich reserves of other minerals enable the region to be a major supplier of raw materials.

The best evidence of the economic dynamism of the region is the emergence of NICs – newly industrializing countries – which have become a model for successful industrialization for Third World countries. Over a twenty-year period, the East Asian and ASEAN countries have realized an average economic growth rate of around 8 per cent, about double the world average. Although this rate may slacken in the 1980s because of new protectionism among the advanced nations and structural imbalances in their own economies, the East Asian countries still have better prospects for economic growth than developing countries in other regions.

As is well known, developing nations and NICs in the Asia–Pacific region have pursued an outward-looking development strategy, and this may have been supported by factors such as social and economic stability, active entrepreneurship, and cheap qualified labour. Asian NICs learned an important lesson from the failure of the import-substitution strategy adopted by some other developing countries since the 1940s. In contrast, export-led growth based on an outward-looking strategy enables developing countries to obtain the foreign exchange needed for their industrialization, and also contributes to the expansion of international trade by inducing imports of more capital goods, equipment and technology from the advanced nations.

In the early 1960s, when Korea launched its first five-year economic development plan and when I served as the Minister of Commerce and Industry, I advocated an export-led growth policy in order to accelerate industrialization. As had been the case in Japan during the 1950s, there were some people who insisted on expanding the import-substitution policy. However, I was convinced that there was no alternative to an outward-looking policy, since we had little capital accumulation after the Korean War and a very narrow domestic market.

This open economic policy naturally generated various negative side effects, such as a growing dependence on advanced economies for both the supply of capital goods and the consumption of export products. The trade deficit has been quite substantial at times, and the trade imbalance between Korea and Japan has not improved yet after more than two decades of active trading between the two countries.

Nevertheless, I still feel that Korea adopted the right development strategy. From the early 1960s to the mid-70s it maintained an average annual economic growth rate of 10 per cent, led by an exceptional export expansion of 40 per cent a year. Even after the oil crisis, when few of the advanced countries could avoid zero or even negative economic growth, the Korean economy grew at an annual rate of between 7 and 8 per cent. Korea became an important presence in world trade, with exports and imports reaching 21,900 million dollars and 24,300 million dollars respectively in 1982.

The other nations in the Asia–Pacific region are either making good progress in terms of economic development, or are at the stage of active planning and implementation. It is imperative, therefore, that we cultivate and intensify the spirit of co-operation amongst ourselves, aiming at the exploitation of every potential we have for the prosperous future of this region.

The need for closer economic co-operation: the role of Japan

The Asia–Pacific region is an area which, for some reason, has hitherto neglected to create any systematic framework for the promotion of regional economic relationships. Western Europe, Latin America, Africa, and several Middle Eastern countries are pursuing such economic integration, and some of the latter groupings are now tied closely to the EEC by preferential trade agreements. In comparison, the Asia–Pacific region has no international organization for economic integration. I should like to stress the urgent need for the establishment of just such an entity to foster economic co-operation in this region.

First, it should be noted that the region is characterized more by complementarity than competitiveness among its members. In fact, the great diversity in factor endowments, economic development, technology, and industrial structure illustrates how we can take advantage of co-operation. For instance, stabilization of the supply of certain strategic natural resources and the effective acceleration of technology transfer would encourage sustained economic growth.

Secondly, one of the ways to overcome the rise in protectionism is to enlarge the market which is all around us and with which we are so familiar. Voices urging protectionism are, unfortunately, growing louder in the capitals of the industrialized countries; they threaten both the NICs and themselves. The structural trade deficit of the Western industrial countries *vis-à-vis* Japan, for example, figures today as one of the most explosive issues.

The recent world economic recession can be classified more as a structural phenomenon than as a mere phase in a cyclical progression, and therefore it is very probable that this new protectionism will become more accentuated. As a result, the need for closer co-operation among the Asia–Pacific nations has become more apparent than ever; this calls for the reduction and elimination of trade barriers and the enlargement of the market.

Thirdly, the near demise of the IMF–GATT system that we have witnessed since the early 1970s provides further proof that the present international economic order can no longer effectively contribute to world trade, as it had done until the 1960s. It is evident that we should make a positive effort to find a method of co-operation, however limited, in the region.

However, despite the fact that closer economic co-operation in the region has become an important issue, we should admit that there exist various obstacles. One of the main problems is the economic disparity that exists between countries in the region. Most of the developing countries are confronted with internal constraints to growth, such as price instability, a shortage of savings, and development imbalances between the economic and other sectors, or between the urban and rural sectors. Moreover, they are faced with balance of payments pressures, a situation which has worsened since the early 1970s, particularly owing to the rise in import prices and the lack-lustre export performance which followed.

In this regard, I should like to stress that Japan, which has become an economic superpower, should take the initiative in bringing about a new Asia–Pacific era. Japan must reconfirm her identity as a nation belonging to Asia, and take the lead in promoting regional co-operation in the knowledge that long-term prosperity in the region will also bring her real gain.

I have witnessed that the expansion of trade can produce substantial gains for the countries concerned, but it should be based on the principle of real equality, and not simply on nominal reciprocity. If this principle is not observed, the gains from trade may be unfairly distributed and the significance of co-operation will be lost.

It is important to bear in mind that the success of economic co-operation will greatly depend on the attitude of Japan, and that the concessions made by advanced countries to the developing countries will, in the long run, lead to mutual prosperity through the expansion of economic transactions.

Most of the developing countries in the Asia–Pacific region have accumulated enormous trade deficits with Japan, resulting in balance of payments difficulties which in turn serve to limit further trade expansion. The role Japan will have to assume in any new era of co-operation should be based on a community spirit and a willingness on the part of Japan to sacrifice immediate benefits for future security and economic expansion throughout the region.

It is now time for Japan to cast a new image among its Asia–Pacific neighbours as a partner who takes the initiative for closer cultural, social, and economic co-operation in the pursuit of common prosperity. This will also serve to inspire the younger generation, teaching them that only active participation on the basis of mutual confidence and interest will bring lasting prosperity.

Some suggestions for a framework for regional co-operation

Despite the fact that trade has increased considerably among the nations of the Asia–Pacific region, a framework is badly needed if we are effectively to foster economic co-operation. I suggest that such co-operation should progress step by step, sector by sector, and that its form should be *sui generis*, unique and relevant to the given circumstances of the region, reflecting mutual interests and equity.

The proposal on Pacific Summitry advanced by President Chun Doo Hwan in July 1982 must be understood in this context. As already mentioned, although there is now this need to intensify co-operation among the nations in the region, we cannot yet envisage the exact form that it will take. Therefore, as President Chun has proposed, the most reasonable course of action is for the top leaders of the Pacific countries to meet for a discussion on matters of mutual concern, and to consult on ways and means for expanding multilateral co-operation.

Of the many areas where co-operation is possible, economic matters can produce real gains for partner countries, since they do not have sensitive implications as do political or military matters.

I personally believe that an advanced form of economic integration – a common market or economic community modelled on the EEC – cannot be realized at this stage, and would not bring any real gains in practice. The Asia–Pacific region consists of countries with enormous economic differences and varying degrees of market intervention, which certainly preclude the possibility of establishing any kind of economic organization in the proper sense of the term.

What matters is to secure the economic sovereignty of member countries and to encourage co-operation and coordination of economic policies. We should pursue such objectives as the efficient allocation of resources, full employment and harmonious economic development, through the expansion of economic transactions, including goods, labour and capital movements, and technology transfer. A mechanism must be designed which takes conditions in the region into consideration.

One of the principles underlying this mechanism would be the promoting of 'agreed specialization' among prospective member countries. This concept is totally different from the economic co-operation attempted by many advanced countries, for example in the EEC. And, because most of the developing countries in the region, including the NICs, consider industrialization to be their first priority, it is preferable that this co-operation should progress on the basis of a horizontal division of labour in the manufacturing sectors, rather than a simple vertical division.

In addition, I should especially like to emphasize that this cooperative framework, if established, must be open to all nations in the region, including countries which, although they may have different economic and political systems, sympathize with our common goal. In fact, a difference in systems does not constitute an obstacle to economic exchanges, and we must hope enthusiastically that all nations in the Asia–Pacific region will align with us in our glorious endeavour.

The strengthening of cultural co-operation

Finally, it should be stressed that such a co-operative framework, although limited to economic matters, cannot function properly unless conditions in other sectors are propitious. As we can see from the example of West European experiences, close economic relations cannot help but influence – and be influenced by – political, social and cultural ties. History teaches us that without solid foundations in other fields economic co-operation cannot succeed and progress will soon come to a halt.

If we hope to promote understanding and co-operation among the interested parties, security and the maintenance of peace in the region are conditions which must first be met. In this regard, I should like to emphasize that for the future of a prosperous Asia–Pacific community, we should organize more exchange programmes in the field of youth training. Our principal task is to explore the path to a new, ideal society, and it is the young generation who should share our goals and make them a reality. We must provide them with favourable opportunities to make wise judgments for a better future.

Most of the Asia–Pacific countries have suffered the trauma of invasion by a foreign race, or of hostile confrontations with other countries in the region. For this reason, they are often inclined to put emphasis on radical nationalism, especially in the education of their youth. Social leaders, including politicians, have neglected to teach the organic function of a state in the international community.

Under such circumstances, if we suddenly emphasize the necessity for close regional co-operation on a basis of equality, young people are likely to become more sceptical, and even confused. Moreover, having been instilled with a sense of superiority, the youth in the relatively advanced countries of the region would experience some conflict in attitudes. In order to prevent this happening we should try to expand youth exchange programmes between countries in the region, and thus provide young people with opportunities to get to know each other, to make comparisons, and to gain an understanding of each country's politics, economics, culture, tradition, and history. This will succeed in inspiring them with the necessity for cooperation.

It is also worth noting that as these young people have not experienced war, the more opportunities they have to know, understand and need each other, the less likely will be the chance of future confrontations occurring between their countries.

Exchange programmes in various fields are now being conducted in the Asia–Pacific region. However, in order to ensure their efficient and systematic execution, they should be organized under a multinational master plan, and supported by private organizations as well as by public agencies.

To provide a suitable preparation for these exchange programmes, it is also desirable that educational curricula – from primary school up to university level – should be improved. For this purpose, we could organize a sort of international curriculum committee for the promotion of education devoted to the Asia–Pacific region.

We should also extend the exchange programmes to various cultural sectors. In fact, I believe that it is time to think of the formation of an Asia–Pacific cultural zone. We have our own original, regional culture based on long historical tradition, and this has served as the cultural foundation of each of our countries. However, this regional culture has many times been disturbed and even pushed aside by Western culture, thus preventing our separate national cultures from attaining harmony with each other. But we are now reaching the state, I believe, when our bright, old culture – of which we should be so proud – is about to blossom. This common culture should serve as the foundation for a new Asia–Pacific era, and as the means whereby we may overcome the constraints facing the nations in the region.

Culture is complex, and it is manifested in many different aspects of a society. Cultural exchanges, therefore, should never be limited to simple transfers of professionals, such as artists, scholars, and intellectuals. What is really required is an organic, functional system by which countries may exchange and evaluate a wide range of knowledge and information in all cultural fields.

In concluding, I should like to emphasize that the world faces a turning-point in its history. The Asia–Pacific region will certainly take a leading role in the coming era, and so we should try to rediscover our identity, and intensify regional co-operation. For the attainment of common prosperity, we must consolidate our foundations and be ready to make immediate sacrifices for long-term gains.

It is our hope that Japan – an economic superpower which occupies a preponderant position in the region – will take a more positive attitude. Times have changed, and the role played by Japan in a future Asia–Pacific era must also change and grow.

Founded 125 years ago, Keio University has done much to fulfil Fukuzawa Yukichi's aspirations by making an important contribution to the emergence of Japan as a world power. It has achieved this by accelerating the implantation of Western civilization and especially by introducing the pioneer's entrepreneurial spirit. Now is the time when the spirit of Keio University should spread not only through Japan, but throughout Asia, and to all the world.

In the pursuit of a mutually prosperous community of nations in Asia and the Pacific, I hope that Keio University will take the lead now and bring Japan back to her rightful place in this community. We look forward to a brighter and happier future.

Japan, from economic power to cultural inspiration?

MOCHTAR LUBIS

Historical background

Japan was not completely unknown to the people of Southeast Asia in ancient times. Some historians have speculated that ancient Malay seafarers reached Okinawa. Before Japanese citizens were forbidden to leave Japan under one of the shoguns' edicts, a small group of Japanese was reported to have settled in Thailand. And in the seventeenth century, the Dutch East India Company recruited Japanese mercenaries to serve with their fleet. When the Dutch conquered the spice island of Banda in the Moluccas, these mercenaries were used to behead captured Bandanese nobles on the deck of the Dutch admiral's ship.

In more recent times, though, as a result of the Japanese army's incursions into East Asia, Southeast Asia and the Pacific, Japan and its people became well known to the inhabitants of those areas. The behaviour of the Japanese military during the Second World War did nothing to recommend Japan to the Indonesians, Malays, overseas Chinese, Burmese, Australians, Filipinos, and others. Understandably, such experiences have created in the region a generally unfavourable image of Japan and the Japanese.

Problems in present relations

Today, a seemingly different kind of Japanese invade Southeast Asia. They no longer wear the old khaki military uniforms; they do not still carry long rifles and samurai swords. Now they come smartly dressed, wearing ties and carrying the ubiquitous

28

attaché case. They come to sign contracts for mineral and timber concessions, fishing rights, foreign investment permits, road-building projects, and factories for cement, textiles, car assembly and electronics. They come as straight investors, as partners in joint ventures. Japanese industrial products have been flooding Southeast Asia. Japanese clubs, restaurants and hotels now dot the cityscapes of the region. Japanese businessmen are back.

Japanese products, such as cars and electronics, have pushed aside many European and American products from the markets of Southeast Asia. American and English automobiles now account for only a very small share of the regional market. What the Japanese had failed to win in the Second World War – access to Southeast Asian natural resources and markets for Japanese industrial products – they have now won through trade, foreign aid, foreign loans, direct investments and joint ventures. But relations between Japan and Southeast Asia are fraught with hidden tensions, some of which are caused by the fact that the Japanese continue to ignore the aspirations and cultural values of the inhabitants of the region.

All nations in Southeast Asia are in the throes of modernizing their societies, and enormous efforts are being devoted to economic development. In all these countries a capitalist free-market economy has developed, modified to some extent by governmental interference in the economy. But whatever modifications are made, most Southeast Asian governments pay at least lip-service to the ideals of social and economic justice. When the Indonesian government came under criticism some time ago, because the fruits of economic development were said to have been poorly distributed, President Suharto tried to soothe public feelings by saying that the people must exercise patience and wait until the cake grows bigger. But very few really believe that the keepers of the big cake will eventually divide and distribute it to others.

In order to stimulate economic development, Southeast Asian governments welcome foreign investments in almost all sectors of the economy. Their basic economic policies are typically based on a capitalistic theory of development, where the target is to increase the GNP growth-rate until the trickle-down effect takes place. It is further hoped that development projects and foreign investments will create many job opportunities.

The experience gained over the last two or three decades has, however, shown that in the developing countries, development within the framework of a mixed-economy policy has – with very few exceptions – in fact increased the gap between the rich and the poor. Many foreign investors prefer to introduce technology that is capital intensive rather than labour intensive; this is to avoid risky confrontations with large numbers of employees. And in many cases Third World governments even go so far as to curb the rights of workers – for example, the right to strike in order to achieve better working conditions – which in the long run naturally leads to tension and bitterness between workers, governments and foreign companies.

Bitterness also results from unemployment. In Indonesia alone about two million young people enter the labour market every year, only a fraction of them finding useful employment. When tensions grow, foreign investors tend to be identified with an oppressive government or blamed for the government's failure to protect the rights of the workers and the interests of the populace.

Many governments in the Third World won initial support from their people on a platform for economic development. National freedom is only a bridge to achieve better living conditions, away from the old poverty and suffering experienced under the colonial powers. But during the struggle for national independence, the people heard other big promises: democracy, the sovereignty and full political participation of the people; respect for human freedom and dignity, social and economic justice, the rule of law; the freedom of expression, of organization, of assembly, and of thought.

However, during the great national push for economic development new factors emerge. In some countries, corruption is rampant. The elite enriches itself and becomes jealous of its vested interests, its position of power and wealth. Members of the elite lose their aversion to the making of alliances with both domestic and foreign entrepreneurs (in Southeast Asia most wealthy, domestic entrepreneurs are overseas Chinese) in order to secure the biggest pieces of the development cake for themselves.

When criticism and opposition grow more vocal and militant, the power elite begins to curb the rights of the people which are constitutionally guaranteed. The more restrictive and oppressive the measures are, the sharper the criticism and the stronger the opposition.

As the opposition grows in strength, so does the reaction of the power elite, which now says that, in order to achieve the goals of development, there is a very great need for stability, continuity and security – for both government and society. Such needs make it imperative that 'press freedom' be given a new interpretation and definition. The freedom and responsibility of the press in a developing society are necessarily different from those in a Western country, or so the people are told. The press is free, but its responsibility is to guarantee stability, continuity and security; its freedom should be used to promote these values for both the government and society as a whole. Journalists who refuse to toe this official line are harassed and arrested, or their newspapers are closed down. In some countries journalists are sufficiently intimidated to practise self-censorship, the most demoralizing situation to be in for any journalist.

The power elite also starts to interfere in the affairs of political parties. To really ensure the continuity, stability and security of the government, the next step is to defuse any political power invested by the constitution in the legislative body, and to neutralize the powers of the judiciary. General elections are manipulated to perpetuate the reign of the power elite. As the press is no longer allowed to reflect the many shades of public opinion or to report the truth, the government itself becomes the captive of its own secret service and informants, who understandably prefer to report only the good news. Government leaders slowly become isolated from social, political and economic realities. In the name of development, the 'developmentalist' regimes in many countries have become repressive and corrupt, an ironic retrogression for societies which have gained independence from colonial repression.

Such is the general process – found in many Third World countries, with local variations – of the change from the idealistic, democratic stage of national independence into authoritarianism and military or civilian dictatorship. The process is still going on today, in many cases abetted and supported by Western democratic and capitalist countries, including Japan. Foreign investors, such as transnational companies, are of course identified with the power elite, and public resentment has been aroused by such things as bribery scandals and the rape of forests.

Today's international economic structure is the creation of the West, and the newly independent countries of the Third World have been – and are still – victims of this structure. The repeated failures of the UNCTAD/North-South dialogues, and the negative response shown to the Third World's demands for a new international economic order only emphasize the unwillingness of the richer countries to co-operate for a new and fairer world.

For many of the intellectuals in the developing countries, the new directions being explored are not a matter of choosing between left and right. Many people in the Third World have been agonizing over the search for their own unique direction, a viable alternative to left and right, a direction which is sustainable within the environment of their own culture and values, their natural and human resources.

Their agony is deepened by the realization that their chances of success depend very much on whether the richer, more powerful industrialized nations are also willing to change, to adopt values other than the classical maximization of profit. It is not only life styles which should change: social, political and economic structures should be reviewed, and philosophies about life and human destiny should be reconsidered.

The agony of young intellectuals in the developing countries represents a radical departure from the lines of thought of the older generation, the generation which today holds power. Many of them accept, without too much questioning, the trickle-down effect of an increasing GNP growth-rate as preached by the IMF, the World Bank, the Asian Development Bank, the transnational companies, the banks and other international agencies. Like the late Shah of Iran, many of them secretly dream of making their country the West Germany or Japan of the Middle East, of East or West Africa, of Southeast Asia or Latin America.

More so than their elders, the young generation in our societies are questioning the validity of the basic concepts of the political and economic systems, social structure and educational system inherited from the colonial past. In Indonesia, the majority of activists in the field of environmental and wildlife protection are young people. Young lawyers are active in legal-aid societies, helping the poor and powerless in their communities to fight for their rights under the law. The movements and organizations in many developing countries which are promoting legal aid, human and consumer rights, environmental protection, women's rights and social welfare, are trying to reach to the grass roots of society. And when they do, the winds of change will certainly blow stronger throughout the Third World.

How then, when we ourselves are embroiled in our own ferment for change, do we perceive Japan and our relations with the Japanese nation?

Perceptions of Japan

I think it would be dangerous to generalize about Southeast Asian perceptions of Japan. Certainly there has been a great change in these perceptions if one compares the pre-war period with the present.

The first favourable perception of Japan arose, I believe, when the Japanese defeated the Russians in the Russo-Japanese War of 1904–5. News of the Japanese victory reverberated through Asia and Southeast Asia like thunder, stirring the hearts and minds of many Asians. For the first time in history an Asian nation had proved that the white people were not invincible. They could be defeated by Asians!

The Japanese victory boosted the self-confidence of Asian nationalists, who hoped that one day they would be able to wrest their freedom from the hands of the imperialist powers. More than anything else, the victory of the Japanese at Port Arthur brought with it a free bonus, a benefit that resulted from no conscious effort on their part: it succeeded in endowing them with a special aura in the eyes of many Asians. Japan gained considerable prestige among the Asian nations, and they in turn gained hope – hope that they might not have to struggle on their own, that the Japanese victor might very well be interested and willing to help them throw off the colonial yoke.

But alas, Japan wanted other things, the same things the colonial powers were after: power, territory, the control of natural resources and markets, strategic bases, etc. When Japan was admitted as a member of the small club of world powers, the bright image of the victor was tarnished. And when it launched its own war of conquest into Manchuria and China, and occupied Korea and Taiwan, Japan became just another imperialist power in the eyes of Southeast Asian peoples – an enemy, a threat and a challenge to their own goal of independence and nationhood.

As the Japanese government grew more and more militaristic and fascist, joining in the Berlin-Tokyo Axis, and then invading the Philippines, the Pacific and Southeast Asia, it became clear to many nationalist leaders in Asia that Japan had become a serious imperialist threat. And in the following years the inhuman behaviour of the Japanese military in Indonesia and elsewhere in Southeast Asia gave rise to bitter feelings of hatred and anger against the Japanese.

But today Southeast Asian perceptions of Japan have again changed, although the basic perception that Japan can still be a threat substantially remains.

This change in perceptions has been caused mainly by Japan's economic performance, and by its successful adoption of Western technology and industrial production methods. These successes have made a deep impression not only in Southeast Asia, but all around the world. Even the Americans and West Europeans are feeling the heat. The French have tried to slow down the influx of Japanese electronic products by such petty means as channelling all such imports through one small customs-house. And the Americans forced the Japanese to curb their automobile exports to the United States by threatening to impose trade restrictions, totally contradicting their declared adherence to free trade.

The economic power of Japan is thus making itself felt in many parts of the world, including Asia. But, at the same time as being aware of Japan's dominating influence on their economies, the industrializing Third World countries are greatly encouraged to see Japan beat the Western industrial powers at their own game. Somehow there is a parallel here, between Japan's recent economic successes and its victory over the Russians at Port Arthur.

As soon as they succeed in penetrating the markets of the West, the industrializing countries of Asia also have to face trade restrictions in the form of tariffs and quotas. Some time ago, Britain imposed a quota on ready-made clothing from Indonesia, causing trade relations between the two countries to sour. But while there is some common ground here, the developing countries find the Japanese really out of their class. In effect, the Japanese belong to the club of rich, highly industrialized nations of the West. Japanese interests lie much closer to the interests of the Western nations than to those of the poorer, developing countries. So, at best, there are mixed perceptions of Japan in Southeast Asia.

When the Japanese, bowing to American pressure, decided to extend their defence reach up to one thousand miles from their shores, there arose among many Southeast Asians – except those in Singapore – immediate cries of alarm and a reawakening of suspicions regarding Japan's real intentions. Adam Malik, former Vice-President of Indonesia, strongly opposed any further increase in Japanese military power, saying that we are very afraid and we hope that Japan will stop rearming.

I still remember the Japan of the years 1950 to 1957, when it was a defeated nation, its big cities destroyed by American bombing, its industries in ruins, its economy in disarray. What is the strength, so deeply embedded in the Japanese nation, that enabled it to rise like a phoenix out of its own ashes to become one of today's great economic world powers?

Japanese cultural continuity

I think the answer must be found in the Japanese culture itself. Japan is well-known for its lack of natural resources. It has to import nearly 100 per cent of its oil and 60 per cent of its coal. It must import iron ore, uranium for its nuclear power industry, and other minerals.

Japan has proved that human resources are more decisive in economic development than natural resources. Why is it, then, that the Japanese can perform this miracle of economic development, while the Indonesians, Filipinos, Thais, Indians, Pakistanis, Malays, Africans and Latin Americans have yet to succeed? Some – like Mexico, Brazil and Argentina – have almost ended up in bankruptcy.

What kind of cultural values cherished by the Japanese enable them to turn defeat into another kind of victory within such a short span of time?

Every visitor to Japan, once he or she steps on Japanese soil, will be impressed that Japanese culture predominates here. This is unlike the situation in many developing countries, where national culture sometimes becomes submerged by alien cultural domination.

The modern technology the Japanese are using is certainly derived from the West, but I can sense that the Japanese have been very successful in adopting and adapting it; they have made it their own, and in many cases improved upon it, in a manner befitting their own genius and creativity.

Although the big Japanese cities with their high-rise buildings look very much like other great cities around the world, when you enter them you immediately sense you are not in New York, Manila or London, but in a Japanese environment.

The borrowing and absorption of foreign cultures has happened constantly throughout human history. The great question is always whether the nation which borrows is able to digest and develop the foreign culture, and whether the original culture consequently gains the strength of creativity. Japan took its script as well as some state institutions and laws from China, and a number of its cultural values from Chinese literature and philosophies.

The Japanese digested elements of Chinese culture to reinforce their own native value system, which was reflected in their feudal hierarchy: very clear differences in status between members of society, and a rigorous code of behaviour between superiors and inferiors, which together resulted in rigid formal attitudes as regards both thought and action. All these were set within the framework of a most rigorous discipline; this flowered especially during the heyday of the Japanese samurai, who lived by the code of bushido.

Shintoism teaches loyalty to the emperor, worship of ancestors, and respect for parents. Shintoism does not teach any concept of sin as taught by Islam and Christianity. The Japanese, therefore, have no sense of the burden of sin.

Two important values in the emotional life of the Japanese are patriotism and loyalty to their emperor. In addition, they have a very strong sense of *giri* – of the 'right reason' or responsibility. To die for the wrong reason is to die like a dog. Real courage means to live for the right reason, and to die for the right reason. Courage means doing what is right. The Japanese owe *giri* to their parents and family, to their superiors, to the emperor, to their nation, and today to the company where they work.

Another strong Japanese cultural value is *renchi-shin* – 'to know shame'. To know shame is the basis for all good traits, good behaviour and morals.

Although the samurai have gone, swallowed by history, their descendants are to be found in new guises: as business entrepreneurs, bankers, industrialists, scholars, lawyers, doctors, engineers, historians, bureaucrats, politicians, labour leaders, artists, writers and journalists. We can see today the old Japanese values reflected in the lifetime employment system, and in the loyalty to one's employer, the company.

When I was in Japan a few years ago, I asked a Japanese friend – one who regards himself as a true democrat and who has studied in the United States of America – whether the emperor is still needed in Japan. Without any hesitation he replied, 'Yes, I think if the emperor is not there, the Japanese will lose something to hold on to.'

The continuity of Japanese culture is like a red thread, going back almost five thousand years into the dim past of Japanese history.

From economic power to cultural inspiration?

New high technologies have now been developed and others are being developed in the advanced, industrialized countries. Japan is also deeply involved in this process, giving the jitters to its American competitors, who see their old industrial and technological supremacy threatened by new Japanese inventions.

The new technological revolution in communications and information, robotics, computers, biotechnology, and alternative sources of energy has brought the world to the threshold of the future and, in some fields, the future is here now, today.

But the future has not arrived at the same moment for all nations of the world. It is not true that the year 2000 is the watershed for a new era, as has been popularized during these last decades.

In some sectors of their society many industrially advanced nations have already entered the future. Of all the nations in the world, Japan is perhaps the most ready to step into the future, with confidence in its ability to cope technologically and economically.

High technologies might very well spur the economies of the industrialized nations to new heights, and assure their continued supremacy and power in the world's economy. The new technology in communications and information, and the marriage of telecommunications with computer technology will give the industrially advanced nations an even greater advantage over the developing countries. They will be able to gather, store, retrieve and disseminate economic intelligence at high speed, enabling them to make decisions much faster than those who are not linked to their communications and information network. I have seen how this new technology works in a few information centres in the United States of America, and I could sense not only its potential and power as an economic weapon, but also its political, military and cultural potential for domination of other societies. On the other hand, used wisely, constructively and with equity for all nations, it also has the potential to be of great benefit to all mankind.

Japan is today engaged in building its own high-technology communications and information system – the CAPTAIN system – and so are the other industrialized nations in the West. Japan is leading in robotics, so much so that a Japanese industrialist once told a Southeast Asian leader that if the Southeast Asian countries cannot catch up fast enough, they might end up with no industry at all. He explained that the robots might reclaim the labour-intensive industries which have been transferred to the developing countries in the past two decades or so, returning them to the industrialized countries from which they came. The robots, he said, create no labour problems, work twenty-four hours a day, and provide products of a consistent quality.

All these new high technologies will certainly give the industrialized nations a greater impetus to move forward, to grow more wealthy and more powerful, and thereby further widen the gap between the rich and poor countries. Needless to say, such development will only increase international tensions around the world, as well as within the developing nations, where power elites make common cause with the powerful transnational companies to the detriment of the poor masses of their people.

It is certain that these high technologies do not guarantee a new era of prosperity and peace for the world. The continued arms race and nuclear war threat still hang above the heads of all nations, and as long as these two great problems remain unsolved, any economic advance will tend to be used to win greater strategic, military and nuclear advantages for the contending power blocs.

It seems to me that, under pressure from the United States, Japan has taken the decision to ally herself with the Western military alliance, and thus limited her own options to act as an independent diplomatic broker in international issues.

I have entitled this paper 'Japan, from economic power to cultural inspiration?' because I have had hopes that Japan might take the leading role in reshaping the present international structure into a new one with built-in equity. I hoped that Japan would be willing to play such a role, because it has the needed cultural values to do so. Though I doubt that there exists the political will among most Japanese to take up this kind of role, I feel it is my duty to give my Japanese friends this message.

What are the cultural elements which might enable the Japanese to develop their nation as a cultural inspiration for a new international environment, a world that is more just and equitable, having more real co-operation and friendship, and structured to solve international disputes and conflicts through peaceful means?

Before we look into this, I should like to point out a pre-condition for establishing this new order, something which should be developed by nations and individuals around the world: the awareness and realization that the present international structure has outlasted its usefulness for most nations in the world. The rich, industrialized nations should also realize that they cannot go on reaching for more and more wealth at the expense of other nations in the world.

I know how difficult it is for nations or even individuals to change their ways. But my travels have brought me face to face with individuals in every continent of the world who have made their own self-transformation into world citizens, have changed their personal values, and developed their own vision for a more humane and just world. So individuals have the potential for change. This is also proved by Nakada Shōichi (see *Look Japan*, 10 June 1983), a Japanese expert who worked in Bangladesh. Based on his experience there, he asked this question: Is it really right for us Japanese to continue in our present situation? The same question has been asked for some years now by individuals in the rich, industrialized societies. Many books have been written about alternative life-styles and development paths. I feel strongly that we should heed the words of Mr Nakada, when he says, '... it is undeniable that if we follow our present path of excess, we will surely meet a catastrophe'. This seems to be in line with a public opinion poll in Tokyo some time ago, when 75 per cent of respondents expressed their wish for a life that is culturally richer, not merely materialistic.

Japan, I feel, can play the role of cultural inspiration for a new international structure because of a number of strong elements in her culture. The first is the Japanese cultural concept of *wa*, harmony. While *wa* was first developed to curb the fierce competitiveness among the Japanese, this concept has taken root in the Japanese attitude towards nature, in their artistic expressions. But so far this concept of harmony is applied only to the Japanese people, their own countryside and their nation. The Japanese take meticulously good care of their mountains, lakes and forests, but do not blink an eye when destroying forests in the Philippines, Malaysia and Indonesia. They have cleaned up the pollution in Tokyo, but continue to pollute the environment in other countries. Can the Japanese extend their concept of harmony to embrace other nations and other countries?

In the same sense, in order to be able to act as cultural inspiration to the world, the Japanese must be able to extend their concept of *giri*, the 'right reason'. With a little modification, this concept of responsibility can be extended to embrace the well-being of all nations.

Another very strong Japanese cultural value is a great sense of national solidarity. This too can be further developed, becoming a sense for international solidarity.

Also traditional is the very close relationship between the Japanese and nature; this could be an inspiration for other industrialized societies to protect more strongly their own environment, and to refrain from destroying the environment of other nations in their greedy quest for natural resources.

Obviously the older generation would not be able to make such radical changes. But when one looks at Japanese demographic figures there is some hope. Fifty-one per cent of the present Japanese population was born after the Second World War. Masuda Yoneji, President of the Institute for Information Society, some time ago made a most interesting analysis of the present young generation in Japan. In general, he said, they have gone through a westernization process, are individualistic and have a scientific attitude. Their ages range from 27 to 35 years. They are able to criticize the emperor, and can distribute leftist publications without being hunted by the police. They are free to see and judge anything, and to say and do what they want. The older Japanese generation has deep cultural ties with China, but the young, post-war generation is cut off from China; this is the result of the American military occupation of Japan, and later because of the break in relations between Communist China and the United States.

Mr Masuda called this young generation the 'MEC generation'. M stands for motorization, meaning they are mobile, quick, free, and aware that they belong to an advanced nation. E is for English, meaning they have an international and cosmopolitan outlook. And C stands for computers, since they possess the ability to digest information and to think. This young generation today accounts for 99 per cent of systems engineers and computer programmers.

And what is the Japanese vision of the future? A number of most interesting views have been expressed in a panel discussion reported in the *Tsusan Journal* of June 1981. One panellist

said that eventually the Japanese will achieve a symbiosis between man and technology. Because Japan cannot survive without technology, the Japanese must develop their art and culture
together with technology, and attempt to create a symbiosis
between them. The creating of a symbiosis between the past
and the future should also be an important goal. When other
panellists asked him what the difference is between symbiosis
and coexistence, he explained that coexistence is the ability to
avoid conflicts by freezing points of confrontation. He further
explained his view that within the framework of politics and
economics the Japanese should work more actively for coexistence with other countries wherever they can do so. Unless
the Japanese succeed in this, there could always be a crisis
which might threaten Japan's own security. In this context
symbiosis is a more positive concept than coexistence.

Another panellist pointed out that today Japan is a great
economic power but has not the capability to set international
standards of conduct. Because of constitutional limitations
Japan cannot become a world leader through military power.
But there is an analogy here with a situation in the past when
Japanese merchants grew rich under the shoguns' power. They
possessed great wealth, yet were powerless politically. But
towards the end of the shoguns' power it seems that they were
able to act more freely, while pretending they were abasing
themselves before the shogun. The panellist then suggested
that perhaps the Japanese can play the same trick in the international community today.

There are already good signs, the first stirrings among
Japanese intellectuals of an attempt to widen their concerns to
other nations. I would certainly not recommend that the
Japanese of today repeat the trick of the wealthy merchants, but
I would support the panellist's suggestion for Japan to participate fully in building a good standard of international conduct
for the nations of the world.

Can the young Japanese generation pull itself away from an
over-fascination with all things Western, and become truer to
the positive values in Japanese culture? Or is the pull of Western culture and technology still too strong for them, and – like
the older Japanese generation – will they continue to think that
the new, industrialized Japan still has to imitate and emulate

Western civilization?

Has not the time come to consider alternatives for the future? As Nakada Shōichi said, 'It is undeniable that if we follow our present path of excess, we will surely meet a catastrophe.' And he is not only speaking for Japan. Actually he is speaking for all of us, for the Indonesians, Chinese, Americans, Germans, Russians, and others. I say this because we just cannot follow the present path of excess: the arms race, the nuclear war threat, the race to control and consume natural resources and markets, the pursuit of more material wealth, and the race for strategic dominance in many parts of the world.

The truth is that today the developing and the developed nations must change, both structurally and culturally.

As I have tried to point out, Japan is in an excellent position to take the initiative in acting as a cultural inspiration for the world.

I believe that man can control the historical process. I further believe we should plan an alternative future, one which can be achieved with the means already available today.

Only when we are able to define for ourselves our own development goals and our own growth philosophies – discarding the capitalist ideas that bigger is always better, and that newer is even better – when we can avoid the technologies of built-in obsolescence, and when we are able to put both our human and economic development within the context of the conservation of the ecological balance in our environment, only then would we have any chance of developing new cultural values that might be really meaningful to human and humane existence in the future. This, I believe, applies to both developing and developed societies.

That is the challenge we face today, that is the challenge I throw at you, the young generation of Japan! Are we all going to go about our daily work, apparently oblivious to these problems, problems which in the end will actually deny us a future?

Can you in the rich industrialized nations really not see the justice in rearranging wealth, political and economic power, both at the international and national levels?

Cannot Japan, for example, see how irresponsible it is towards human life in the whole world when she plans to dump radioactive nuclear waste between Japan and the northern

Mariana Islands in the Pacific, as proposed by the Japanese Science and Technology Agency? I should like to refer you to an article in the *Asian Wall Street Journal* written by the biologist Jackson Davis of the University of California, in which he states that the ocean is probably the worst place on earth to put radioactive waste: it is a formidable environment that makes mockery of human structures such as 'radioprotective' containers. Experience with the dumping of radioactive waste off the California coast has shown that radioactivity leaking from the containers can enter the seafood chain. Moreover, a study indicates that low-level radiation, in amounts that might be expected to enter fish from the dump sites, may be more hazardous to health than anyone previously imagined. That is warning enough for anyone!

Conclusion

After all the challenges I have thrown at you, the young generation of Japan, I feel it is my duty to contribute some suggestions as to how we can meet these challenges in the spirit of friendship and co-operation, helping each other as we walk together into a better human future.

I hope that Japan can keep herself free from any kind of entanglement in the present confrontation and arms race between the superpowers and their military alliances. Because only by being a free, independent economic power can Japan – if it has the inclination and determination to do so – develop as a source of cultural inspiration for the world.

The next step would be for Japan to take the initiative and participate in ventures which transcend different ideologies, and which I believe should not raise problems for co-operation between nations in the world. Among such ventures are the following:

- Investment in the development of human resources, concentrating not only on the teaching of skills or education in science and technology, but also on the new cultural values that human kind needs for the future.
- Establishment of a new international mechanism for trade

that will really serve all nations; included would be the reform of or creation of international institutions, such as GATT.

- Adaptation of technologies to make them answer the needs of various nations, and the sharing of sophisticated technologies when they are really appropriate for a given situation.
- Joint international research to solve pressing problems in the fields of energy, agriculture, medicine, post-harvest technology, food security, soil conservation, forest and wildlife preservation, marine farming, biotechnology (in order to lessen modern agriculture's dependence upon oil-based fertilizers and herbicides), and soil improvement or land regeneration using biological methods.
- Taking the initiative to organize an international think-tank to formulate new insights and ideas for the constitution of a more just international community. The United Nations University in Japan can perhaps organize such a think-tank.
- Establishment of international gene banks to improve the quality of both plants and animals.
- Taking the initiative to organize joint international research into alternative sources of energy, especially solar energy. If, for example, OTEC (Ocean Thermal Energy Conversion) technology could be made sufficiently economical, those countries with access to the tropical seas could become energy producers.

As I have said, I do not feel optimistic about the ability of nations to change their ways quickly, if ever, unless they are threatened by imminent catastrophe. Even this is problematical, because – right up to the very last moment – nations tend to believe that somehow they can squeeze through any crisis. If it had not been for the dropping of the atomic bombs, the Japanese might have continued to resist the American invasion of the Japanese islands. The willingness of the kamikaze pilots to carry out their death missions against the American fleet was a grim portent of what might have happened.

As much as the world needs new cultural values to build a better community, our own old cultures weigh heavily upon us, making change a very slow and agonizing process.

Today, around the world we see more ominous signs of war and conflict; the arms race continues unabated, and none of the superpowers has shown any willingness to pause and reflect on the need to reorganize the handling of world community affairs in a much more sane and humane way.

There is fear around the world today, a high sense of insecurity about the present and the future. No nation has yet provided an example of how to bring about really basic changes in the structure of its international relations and commitments. Our commitments are still to compete for more power and more wealth for our own country, just as our power elite competes for its own interests.

This, then, is the challenge I throw to you, the young generation of this mighty economic empire – Japan. Will you, and can you, take your nation beyond the confines of a mere economic superpower to become a source of cultural inspiration for the whole world? Can you prove, by your actions inside Japan and by your relations with the other countries of the world, that you can act sanely, with more human compassion, with more courage to hold high moral and human values, and more justice in your dealings with other nations, expecially with the weaker and more fragile nations of the Third World?

If you can do so, I assure you that many nations will join with you in stepping together towards a better future.

How can Japan contribute to a more peaceful and prosperous world?

SUZUKI TAKAO

How 'small' a country is Japan?

One of the things you hear many Japanese saying these days, almost as if it were someone's pet phrase, is that 'after all, Japan is a small country'. There certainly cannot be very many non-Japanese who have heard a Japanese use the word 'big' of his country. As we see it, not only is the total area of land small and natural resources extremely scarce, but even self-sufficiency in supplying food has proved quite an intractable problem. Add these up and you get the answer that Japan is a 'small' country.

With regard to geographical area, it is a fact that we have only one twenty-fifth of the land area of the United States. And France, which is but a small corner on one of the smaller continents of the world, has double the territory of Japan.

The story for natural resources is a similar one: there are no domestic supplies of high-grade coal or iron ore, and at present 90 per cent of our petrochemical energy comes from abroad. Here again, it is no surprise that most Japanese should think of their nation as less than 'big' or 'major'.

However, we have to be careful about how we interpret these facts. To conclude, for example, that 'smallness' in this sense means that Japan is a weak nation – a weakling on the international scene – is a serious mistake. It has been true enough – especially in the past – that large and richly endowed nations have been the powerful ones, and that 'small' was virtually synonymous with 'weak'. But, in the world as it exists today, it is no longer true that size and resources equate with power.

There seems to be a size beyond which it becomes difficult to manage a nation economically. Expansive territories make for tremendous expense in constructing and maintaining railroads

47

and highways, and this can be a drain on the economy. Small in terms of area, Japan conversely has coastlines which exceed those of the United States in length. This means ideal natural conditions for industrial development along the coasts, which in turn all but obviates the necessity for large-scale overland transportation.

Over-population is another example of how greater size is not necessarily beneficial. It often happens that over-population impedes a nation's development because of the problems it creates in food supply and related areas. Finally, even natural resources do not make a country strong if conditions are such that they cannot be taken from the land because of under-population, unfavourable climatic conditions, or geographical impediments.

Despite these discrepancies in the small=weak, large=strong equation, the average Japanese naively persists in the commonsensical view that Japan is not one of the powers on the international scene because it is 'after all, a small country'.

But if we define a nation's strength in terms of the degree of influence it exerts on other nations, Japan is anything but a weakling. An objective assessment of the present-day state of affairs suggests that Japan ranks among the superpowers. While barely accounting for just 2 per cent of the global population, the Japanese are responsible for more than 10 per cent of the world's economic activity.

Trends that arise among the Japanese – the choices and decisions implemented – have immediate and profound effect on various facets of the world's political economy. In this sense, there is simply no way Japan can avoid 'making waves'. It is this state of affairs that is behind the by now common description of Japan as an 'economic superpower'. There are at present approximately 160 nations on the face of the globe, but there are no more than four countries or areas that warrant the term 'economic superpower': the United States, the Soviet Union, the European Economic Community, and Japan. Like it or not, there we are.

*Is it possible for a pacifist nation
to become an economic superpower?*

This brings us to an important point. In our world today, we find ourselves more than ever before living in a web of inter-dependence. Given such a context, the fact that wealth is concentrated in the hands of so few nations can only result in friction, confrontations and tensions between them and the overwhelming majority of other countries, so far their economic inferiors. The logic behind this is simple: when a pie of a certain limited size is to be divided up among a number of people, and a few individuals take most of it for themselves, there is less remaining for the others, and they naturally feel less than pleased about it.

It therefore behoves us Japanese first of all to realize that, regardless of whether or not a nation's individual citizens plan-ned such an outcome, when they end up with most of the pie, their nation looms large, threatening and unpleasant in the eyes of neighbouring countries. As things stand now, Japan appears to the world – and especially to its Asian neighbours – as an all-too-big nuisance.

Severely defeated in the last war, Japan discarded all inten-tions of aggression, renounced war as a means of resolving international disputes, and declared that it would not even maintain armed forces. Thus reborn as a pacifist nation, it has, in the interests of being a good neighbour, steered hard by the light of non-aggression. In the process, Japan has compiled the admirable record – unique among the major powers – of not having become directly involved in any armed conflict during the forty years since World War II ended.

During this time the Japanese have given themselves up wholly to the job of resurrecting a devastated society and economy. What is more, and worthy of emphasis, is the fact that every one of the goods they produce and sell to the world was made for peaceful use. Even France, which most Japanese consider to epitomize cultural and artistic accomplishment, earned the immense sum of 41,000 million francs in 1982 from the sale of weapons abroad. This makes France the world's third largest exporter of military hardware, surpassed only by the United States and the Soviet Union.

When you consider that for almost forty years now, the Japanese have singlemindedly pursued an economic policy that excludes the sale of military goods, that they have had nothing to do with aggression or other means of disrupting peace in the world, it stands to reason that they think of their nation as a pacifist one. As I see it, however, those Japanese who share this view are fundamentally mistaken.

There is a movement afoot in Japan today to increase armaments, so as to be prepared to resist the threat of aggression from abroad. In response, there are also a good many people who have vowed steadfast opposition to such rearmament, which they see as a return to the militarism of the past, a serious blunder that could drag not only the Japanese, but people of other nations as well, into a tragic armed conflict.

I cannot go along with either of these views, for the reason that both are content simply to oppose each other with regard to the question of how Japan might most profitably maintain its present life-style and extravagant level of consumption. That there might be something wrong with the 'economic miracle' itself is a question that does not even occur to them. There are some 120 million Japanese for whom the pursuit of the good life – or a better life – is a matter of course, regardless of the goods and resources that might be squandered in the process.

I am convinced that there is no just way we can let this unchecked pursuit of higher consumption and materialistic extravagance go on. Whether one looks at it from the perspective of human history or in terms of the problem of how to distribute the world's wealth and resources fairly among its 5,000 million inhabitants, there is no approving such a policy.

To be sure, the Japanese are not the only guilty party; the industrialized nations of the West are equally reprehensible, if not more so. But no matter whom we blame, there is no ignoring the threat: this manner of living, and the social and economic mechanisms erected on such a criminal waste of energy and resources may well inflict irreparable damage on the ecosystems of our globe. Humans will not be the only losers. Above and beyond this, is the hard question of whether such reckless pursuit of material progress will result in real human happiness, or whether we humans have really become any happier or wiser over the years. There is no way the people of Japan and a handful of Western nations can expect to go on enjoying an almost profane life of luxury and indolence while millions – often as close as 'next door' – lack basic medical care and food supplies. It is inhumanely unfair.

This is what I had in mind in stating earlier that both the conservatives and progressives are equally mistaken in the premiss that underlies their respective arguments: that continued pursuit of material prosperity is only natural and hardly something to feel uneasy about.

In the minds of most people, the words 'aggression' and 'incursion' conjure up images of war or military expansion. But economic aggression is every bit as reprehensible. In fact, in the final analysis, what is the purpose of most wars if not to gain economic advantage and an easier life for one's own group, at the expense of another group? War, then, is not an end in itself, but one means of attaining economic prosperity. And so, if one thinks of war as a necessary expense in the pursuit of prosperity, it turns out that Japan has succeeded over the past forty years in securing the prosperity while avoiding the burden of heavy military expenditure.

Now if this is a prize the Japanese have won entirely through their own hard work, with no help from anyone, without stepping on anyone's toes or imposing any burdens on other countries, then there is no problem. To prosper without spending any money on armaments, or going to war, is only what a man would wish for his country, and this makes Japan a model country. Or does it? One wonders, for instance, if the nations surrounding Japan, whose interests are directly connected with Japan's, think of us in this way.

Major powers: roles and responsibilities

As I have indicated, a major power like Japan has certain international responsibilities, which follow from the fact that the things it does or fails to do have untold effects throughout the world. First of all, a major power must possess an accurate awareness of itself as seen from without, and an objective sense of its strength in particular.

At the same time, a major power must be prepared to assume

the difficult role of standing and acting on its own, of making the first move – not acting passively in response to circumstance, or as the necessity arises, but actively, on the basis of judgments grounded in careful information-gathering and an accurate assessment of the world situation. For a major power, there is none of the security that comes from living in the shadows cast by other nations, and no more of the advantages of maintaining a low profile. Of course, should a major power act on a mistaken assessment of the situation, or a wilful preconception, it can wind up not only damaging its own interests, but in wreaking havoc on other nations as well. What all this boils down to are the basic prerequisites for a major power: a thoroughgoing capacity for gathering information domestically and abroad, accurate analysis of the same, and competent judgment in deciding what course of action to take.

So far, I have stressed the idea that the Japanese are not sufficiently aware of the status of their country as a major power. But I do not mean such urging as an attempt to stir other Japanese to stand up, chests out, and take pride in their heritage. What I am after is the realization that insofar as Japan is an established economic power, it is necessary that it makes the effort to know what it looks like from the outside; what we need is an effort, on a national scale, to improve the system with which we gather information, so that we may shape our idea of present world conditions from factual reports and knowledge, not from illusions and preconceptions. But what we have at present, thanks to the lack of awareness of the influence Japan wields in the world, is – I may say without fear of exaggeration – not a nation rich in information and knowledge about itself and the world, but a country so lacking in these that it is virtually shut in on itself. The situation resembles that of a giant, big and mighty, who has gone blind and deaf; he becomes, if anything, a dangerous nuisance. At present, as I see it, this virtual seclusion from the flow of information is Japan's single greatest defect.

Japan – an information-deprived superpower?

There is nothing at all about the existing political and social frameworks in Japan that has to hinder either the exchange of information with people of foreign countries or the expansion of cultural exchange with them. NHK and many other Japanese radio and television broadcasting companies have cast a wide network of news bureaus over the globe, and our newspapers also maintain branch offices in virtually every corner of the world. Every day, countless telephone calls and telexes are sent back to Japan by reporters and other Japanese stationed abroad, in hot competition with one another, producing a data glut so great as to defy handling. And then, of course, there are short-wave radio and the foreign press – broadcasts, newspapers and magazines available to anyone who wishes to listen or subscribe, and establish his own direct contact with the world outside Japan. Perhaps the most direct method is to take oneself abroad for a first-hand look. Here too, anyone who wants to go is free to do so. In 1982, some 4.7 million Japanese did just that, and roughly 3 million people came to visit Japan.

Moreover, when it comes to voicing one's opinion it seems that Japan may well be the freest nation on earth. You can disparage the government or criticize the imperial family and no one will punish you. You can leak an important government secret, and the act itself will not be held against you. Or you can shout out at the top of your voice, urging the dissolution of Japan as we know it, and no one will stop you.

At least in terms of the constraints imposed by the system itself, Japan enjoys a greater degree of liberty, equality and openness than even France, birthplace of the freedom of speech, or the United States, the original 'democratic experiment'. If Japan is this free and this open, you may well doubt my sanity when I claim, as I have, that Japan is an 'information-deprived' nation, a superpower shut in upon itself. I believe, however, that when you hear my reasons for thinking so, you will agree that it is a valid characterization.

Japan: uninterested and woefully uninformed about the rest of Asia

Many of you no doubt recall the uproar that occurred in the mass media in 1982 over the selection of the site for the 1988

Olympics. Japan had proposed Nagoya, while South Korea had put forward Seoul. The incident that created such a stir was the final vote. Right until the day of the announcement, all newspapers, radio and television stations in Japan covered the story in such a way as to suggest that Nagoya had already been picked as the site. Not a single commentator so much as hinted that Seoul just might be chosen.

People in Nagoya took this coverage at its word, and believing the decision to be a sure thing, pushed ahead with printing and building plans, despite the fact that no announcement had been made. Since Nagoya's selection was regarded as all but decided, the evening of the announcement saw television stations all over Japan ready and waiting to break the good news. But the voting nations voted for Seoul and not for Nagoya, by the wide margin of fifty-two to twenty-seven.

The news that Seoul had won plunged the networks into utter confusion, and the coverage on television that night was almost too pitiful to watch. Next morning, the dailies, similarly shaken, reported that the selection finally made was completely unexpected and had caught everyone off guard. One hears that two hundred or more Japanese reporters and sports representatives had thronged to Baden-Baden, where the International Olympic Committee was meeting. And one wonders what in the world they were up to while such a 'completely unexpected' decision was in the making.

As we later learned, the South Korean delegation had rounded up enough votes to be sure of a decision in favour of Seoul by as early as a week before the selection committee actually sat down for the final show of hands. This means that the South Korean diplomats, reporters and sports representatives must have mounted a concerted and intense campaign to win over the delegates from other nations. How could it be that not a single one of the two hundred Japanese on the scene caught wind of this? The reasons may run something like this: first of all, it is doubtful that anyone ever took Seoul to be a site capable of serious competition with Nagoya; also at work, no doubt, was the arrogant notion that a major power like Japan would never be bypassed in favour of the likes of South Korea. Seeing only what they expected to see, the reporters came up with no news worthy of the name.

Another reason why the Japanese press corps failed to pick up on the campaign mounted by the Korean delegation is that there was not a reporter among them who could speak Korean, or who ever had an interest in Korean affairs. Since I have not conducted a survey, I cannot state this categorically, but for reasons which I shall mention shortly, it at least seems quite unlikely that there were any Japanese in Baden-Baden who could speak Korean. As it happened, this incident turned out to expose the fact that we Japanese, even today, remain un-interested in making a serious effort to learn anything – language, culture, or thought – about South Korea. Consequently, as the incident showed, the sad fact is that we are incapable of acquiring accurate information about our nearest neighbour.

A problem of precisely the same nature occurred three years ago when the construction of the Baoshan steel works in China was suddenly called off. Just after the Japanese had agreed to build a mammoth modern steel works there, and to invest the immense sum of 200,000 million yen, word came from the Chinese that owing to insufficient preparation they were not ready to start construction on the project. When this news reached the Japanese they were completely taken aback, and straightening the matter out cost them dearly; they had failed to anticipate or even consider such a turn of events.

How could it happen that the Japanese side did not investi-gate and find out, before contracting, whether or not it would be possible to start right away on construction of the works? Is this not China, a country with whom Japan has enjoyed cultural exchange for two thousand years? Our peoples are of the same racial stock, use the same script – a close relationship extolled in Japan, it seems, at every opportunity – and yet we can be caught completely unawares. Why are we for ever starting something, only to be greeted with the familiar phrase 'Due to unforeseen developments, matters are at present being reconsidered'? It is all because Japan is still shut in on itself – an information-deprived superpower, one of the wonders of the modern world.

As I have suggested, there are no physical obstacles or hind-rances built into our socio-political system to render the gather-ing of accurate information impossible. The problem lies instead with us, in our hearts and minds, the way in which we see things. As the Bible says, a man may 'look', but if his heart is not in it, he will not 'see'. There is a strong tendency in Japan today to see only the things we want to see, and to hear only what we want to hear. There is an unwillingness to look calmly and objectively, and to collect and report news that is unpleasant or less than flattering.

It all too easily happens that the facts about an unpleasant subject are either ignored or underestimated, with preconceived notions taking precedence. Or, in the case of a popular topic, an extremely favourable view is taken, wishful thinking filters out the unpleasant elements, and everything comes out rose-coloured.

As I see it, this lack of reportorial acumen on the part of Japan, and its tendency to take the affairs of non-Western nations all too lightly, stem from serious gaps in our social and political mind-set. The Foreign Ministry's confusion several years ago when, against all expectations, Japan failed in its bid to be nominated as one of the UN Security Council's elected members, may be traced to the same shortcomings, as may the way in which the press handled the revolution in Iran, the collapse of the Iran–Japan joint petroleum venture, and the assassination of the Egyptian President Sadat.

But, on the other hand, when it comes to information about Europe and the United States, we are up to our necks in any and every kind of news – certainly more than we need. I should like to discuss why this should be so.

'Japanese spirit, Western learning'

In the latter half of the last century, when the Japanese finally shed the hard, thick shell of two hundred and fifty years of isolation, they were profoundly impressed with the marvellous accomplishments of Western science and technology, which were being introduced into Japan one after the other. The leading men of the day, who set out without a moment's delay to observe this foreign civilization at first hand, were especially taken with the great cities of the West; street after street of tall, stone houses; well-paved, broad avenues; and well-dressed citizens. Breathing in the fullness of this prosperity, it seemed to them that the very air was suffused with the light of civilization.

'Japan has fallen behind. We can't go on like this. Japan may not be exactly backward or primitive, but if we're going to call the West "civilized", then Japan is "semi-civilized". Something has to be done, and fast, to civilize and enlighten our land.' It was with thoughts like these enshrined in their hearts that the Japanese leaders returned, one by one, from abroad.

These men were inspired with the strength and charm of the cultures and civilizations of Europe and America, which they took as Japan's models when they plunged into their effort to modernize. But there was more behind this move than the simple desire to emulate.

As they travelled through Asia and Africa on their way to Europe, they were also struck with a sense of severe crisis. Most of the lands they stopped in were under European control, either as colonies or protectorates, and they saw with their own eyes the wretched state of submission in which the peoples of those lands lived. Caught napping, and Japan too could lose its independence and be turned into a European colony. There was no time to lose in casting off the heavy, stagnant traditions of the Orient: to stand up to the West, one first had to learn from it. The idea was to fight fire with fire.

This notion of westernization as a means for Japan to preserve its independence and autonomy, so that its citizens might deal with the people of Western nations on an equal basis, was caught rather well in the oft-used phrase *wakon yōsai*, or 'Japanese spirit, Western learning'. In these words you can almost feel the mettle of those men and see them standing up to a monster they feared might at any moment swallow them whole, in the hope that they could learn to grow equally strong.

Now that the terrible wounds inflicted by Western colonization have long since healed over, from our international perspective today it is easy enough to dismiss the thinkers of the Meiji enlightenment and their slogans – like *datsua nyūō* ('Quit Asia, look to the West') advocated by our university's own founder, Fukuzawa Yukichi – as so much blatant egoism. But anyone with a smattering of knowledge of actual conditions during the latter part of the nineteenth century – when 'law of the jungle' and 'survival of the fittest' were also phrases that described Asia's plight under the yoke of Western colonization – will most likely see the 'Quit Asia' policy pursued by Japan as an unavoidable counter-measure. As in the game of chess, sac-rificing some of your pieces, even valuable ones, can ensure that you at least stay in the game, and in control of your own moves.

Be that as it may, it is a fact that the lack of interest and know-ledge about Asia that still persists among most Japanese today has its roots in the modernizing policies of Meiji Japan, when the seeds sown were exclusively the imported, Western variety. Today, a century later, this bias in our planting has become a distinct disadvantage: a society has grown up with no place for an Asian perspective.

As an example of how a tendency to ignore the other nations of Asia is built into things, I should like to relate to you a telling little anecdote. The Japanese Ministry of Education has tradi-tionally sent promising young people abroad so that they might pursue new intellectual developments and master the latest and best in technology. For a long time – too long – the ministry's policy did not recognize Asian countries as permissible loca-tions for study abroad, which is tantamount to saying that there is nothing to be learned in a 'backward place like Asia'. On one occasion, when a scholar specializing in oriental architecture applied for support in order to study somewhere in Asia, the ministry treated the case as an exception, and granted condi-tional approval. And that condition, believe it or not, was that the grantee had to pass through a Western nation on his way back from his actual place of study. Laughable and silly as it may seem, this anecdote throws into striking relief the Japanese formula for success at modernization: make catching up with the West the national objective, in the interests of efficiency and speed, clearly limit all activities to this target, and then work like a horse.

It is plain enough, without my pointing it out, that Japan's present prosperity is inseparably linked with Asia at all points on the political and economic game board: resources, trade and security, to name a few. In principle, at least, the fact that Asia, in this broad sense, is very important to Japan is something all Japanese should admit to, just as Japan is a presence the rest of Asia cannot ignore. So how can so many of us continue to sit back calmly, no more curious than before to learn about things Asian? Why does this appalling ignorance and lack of interest persist? To give the simplest answer, it is because the Japanese do not feel any strong attraction for Asia. Far from feeling some kind of attraction, many Japanese feel something more akin to disdain or aversion. How, one asks, did such a state of affairs ever come about?

The psychology of contempt

Although Japan has had the experience of invading other countries, the Japanese themselves – with the exception of the Okinawans – are a people without the experience of full-scale invasion or brutal subjugation at the hands of another nation which has turned their country into a battlefield. This means that they have never had a foreign culture forced upon them. Japan was defeated and occupied by the United States but, as it turned out, this passed without leaving any festering wounds or deep-seated animosity in the hearts of most Japanese.

Consequently, the whole process of being influenced by a foreign country has taken on an interesting form in Japan. Without exception, this process takes place on the initiative of the Japanese. The result is that we acquire what we ourselves think is interesting or attractive in a foreign culture; the yardstick applied reflects our own criteria of worth, our own aesthetic sense, and the choices are our own too. We pick up only on those things that appeal to us as Japanese. That which we dislike, consider inferior, or that which does not match our tastes, is ignored. No doubt this happy condition, whereby we choose what comes into the country and import only what we really desire or prize, has contributed to the fact that anti-foreign sentiment does not take root in Japan – a somewhat unusual state of affairs. In fact, nothing could be further from anti-foreign sentiment than Japan's love affair with ancient China, or the more recent relationship with the West – situations where Japan has beautified and idealized the objects of its affection far in excess of their actual merits, and developed what I have called the 'mirage effect'.

Cultural change that takes place in this way, without invasion or conquest, means that the general public has no direct contact with people from other countries, and that cultural exchange is conducted exclusively through the few in the front lines: diplomats, scholars, religious men, and merchants. Since these people set out for their respective destinations with the express purpose of finding and bringing back only what will go over well in Japan, the average Japanese has come to think, for example, that ancient China and Europe were veritable treasure-houses chock full of nothing but the best things on earth. And the inhabitants of these marvellous lands were similarly conceived: an educated, morally upright race of handsome men and beautiful women.

In short, beyond the sea lay an earthly paradise with no defects and nothing of inferior quality, a Utopia realized in the form of China and Europe. This is the mirage effect, which I have suggested arises when a foreign culture is absorbed indirectly.

Thanks to the intensity of this mirage effect, the further modernization has progressed in Japan, the more people have tended to regard the West as a sort of heaven on Earth, and this has resulted in a dominant view that is completely uncritical of the West. In fact, the Japanese of the Meiji period were more impartial and flexible than we in their evaluation of things Western, interested as they were in westernization as a tool, rather than as an object in itself. Guided by a clear awareness of differences in historical background and social structure, their approach was a relativistic one, which admitted first of all that 'Customs will differ from place to place'. This pragmatic attitude left them enough leeway to pick and choose in a free, unbiased way. However, as time went on, a firm and uncritical belief in Western culture took root. From this perspective, anything, if it came from the West, had to be better than the time-honoured native tradition.

Of course, various kinds of resistance to this tendency have sprung up, including movements of a reactionary or ultra-nationalistic nature. But on the whole, the tendency has been in favour of uncritical 'Western-centrism', an attitude which has come to dominate the hearts and minds of most Japanese. Of all societies mankind has fashioned, that of the West is seen as the most progressive, and the one most fully evolved. Absolute superiority on the part of the West is seen not just as an advantage in the natural sciences or industrial technology, but as something which extends through all spheres of social life, from morality and religion, to philosophy, and even literature.

Given this kind of mental climate, the Japanese are elated when it seems they have caught up with the West or moved ahead, but disappointed and dejected when they feel they have fallen behind. Spirits rise and fall with each image reflected in the eternal mirror of the Western standard. Here, I submit, is the reason why Japan has for so long been so little interested in Asia, and made scarcely a move to get to know its neighbours, despite occasional lip-service to the contrary. This attitude follows from the way in which other Asian countries appear to the Japanese. What Japan has bravely resolved to discard, other Asian nations seem still to cling to; they appear to be stuck deep in the mud of age-old non-Western traditions, from which Japan has managed to pull herself free only with the greatest effort.

In the years following the Meiji Restoration, the educational system that was drawn up in order to implement the national policy of 'Quit Asia, look to the West' was of course quite European in its design and intent, and there were virtually no provisions made for the cultivation of knowledge about Asia. The best illustration of this bias is the imbalance in the languages one can study at school in Japan. As things stand at present, there are almost no opportunities to learn an Asian language at junior or senior high-school level, and even at university level only a few Asian languages are offered at a handful of institutions.

On this point, it is pleasing to note that the progressive foreign-language programme at Keio stands among the top two or three programmes in all of Japan. In addition to English, French and German – which you can learn almost anywhere in Japan – courses are available in such languages as Russian, Chinese, Spanish, Korean, Classical Greek and Latin. And, if so inclined, you can take advantage of the instruction available through the Institute for Language and Cultural Studies, and the Attached School of Foreign Languages, to learn such Middle Eastern languages as Arabic, Persian, Turkish, or Southeast Asian languages like Burmese, Thai, Indonesian, Vietnamese. However, given the present circumstances, most of these languages that one may broadly describe as 'Asian' are available only as electives, after a student has fulfilled his basic requirements in Western languages – English, German or French. Consequently, there are very few students who actually enrol for Asian languages. What I would like to see, and what I think we need, is a foreign-language programme more capable of responding to Japan's present position and status in the world, a programme in which, say, a student receives instruction in one Western language and one Asian language.

The creation of such a programme would, of course, require that we reform the present one considerably. Just as Fukuzawa Yukichi's Keio contributed greatly to Japan's modernization by providing the country with scores of men highly skilled in English, so too, in the years ahead, I should like to see Keio play an active role in guiding Japan back to a more balanced awareness of its place and status in the world, by producing young men and women who are competent in Asian languages, and well-versed in the culture, history and natural features of the countries of Asia.

The need to break away from Western-dominated thought

As the remarks I have made so far suggest, we can view the disappearance of the rest of Asia from Japan's intellectual horizon as the high price it paid in order to secure the fruits of modernization, which in actuality was just another name for westernization. From the Meiji era down to the present, the rest of Asia was removed from the field of vision, so as to concentrate better on the object of emulation, the industrialized West. And so the serious problem we are faced with today is how to make the picture whole again, how – without further delay – to restore an essential component too long absent. The advantages that come with a stable relationship, built on mutual understanding and a readiness to co-operate, would not only benefit the countries directly involved – Japan and its Asian neighbours – but would also make a significant contribution to peace and prosperity in the world at large.

While it may seem like a rather roundabout route to take, if we Japanese are ever going to develop a real interest in the rest of Asia, we must first break the spell we cast on ourselves when we swallowed the notion of across-the-board Western superiority. The unnnatural and unnecessary idealization of the West resulting from the 'mirage effect' has produced an idol that we can no longer afford to worship. Only by destroying this idol can we clear a place in our hearts where feelings of affinity with the rest of Asia can spread their roots and grow. First, we must wake up to the lack of absolute values among the great variety of human cultural institutions, and develop a selectively critical attitude with regard to things Western. Only then can we hope to realize that, far from warranting dismissal, Asian ways and values can provide effective, and even superior alternatives or supplements to Western ways, as we humans attempt to cope with the many problems in our world today. Only through such an expanded awareness, in combination with a sense of affinity and solidarity with the rest of Asia, will we ever know the confidence and joy that come with the realization that our way of life and traditions have much to contribute to mankind.

Destroying the occidental idol we have set up in our hearts is thus a prerequisite for developing a real dialogue with the other nations of Asia. But this act is significant for Japanese in another way as well. Allow me to explain. Until just ten or twenty years ago, Japan's relationship with the West could be described, in most respects, as a vertical one: the nations of the West clustered at the top, with Japan on a lower level. The Japanese response, of course, was to rouse the entire nation in an all-out effort to rise from the depths; we studied our Western models assiduously, choosing everything of promise for introduction into Japan. The effort succeeded, and we have pulled up level with the West.

The turning-point can be described as a sudden shift in the axis of comparison from vertical to horizontal. Japan and its former Western models are now competitors in the same division and in the same ring. The problem with this sudden and dramatic change in the relationship, however, is that neither the Japanese nor the people of Western nations have managed to shift mental gears quickly enough; thus, accurate data and mutual understanding have lagged behind. In other words, the friction over trade and other economic confrontations that have arisen are actually better understood as the result of two cultures bumping clumsily against one another.

The problem came about when the lone non-Western nation,

Japan, began to perform rather well on a stage that had always been dominated by Western players, who had written the original scripts, chosen the settings, and set the standards by which a performance was to be judged. All went well until Japan stepped out of line and succeeded in upstaging the rest while following its own script. What this amounted to was the realization that the happy ending – beauty, strength, and happiness – could be attained just as well with one plot as with another. The Western monopoly of the global theatre was broken, and, it would seem, the standards for successful 'productions' rewritten.

Now, this success of ours is the product of a combination of Western ideas and elements native to our culture. Japanese today do not, by any means, behave like Westerners. And while the goods we produce – like our society, or our ways of thinking – cannot be described as oriental in any traditional sense of the word, these are not cast from Western moulds either. If there is something attractive about Japan, if there is something about Japan's products that appeals to the people of other nations, it is surely none other than this quality that is neither exclusively Western nor exclusively oriental.

To return to that Western idol that we have set up in our hearts, and the need to drive it out: as I have contended, unless we do so, we cannot break free of the deluded notion that our worth and our successes are to be decided in terms of how well we measure up against Western standards. As long as the relationship with the West actually was a vertical one, the fascination and adoration were all very well. In such a situation, a 'love is blind' approach works quite well; one need not recognize the faults and shortcomings in the object of one's emulation. After all, it is not these shortcomings that one is interested in making one's own. At this stage of the relationship, what one is after are those items of quality lacking in oneself. And so Japan imported such items, in order to modernize. Since research was directed to these ends, and not to gaining an objective, accurate picture of what the West was really like, there was little harm in adopting an adulatory attitude.

But now that the relationship is no longer a vertical one, now that Japan competes on an even footing with its former mentors, the attitude that only idealizes, ignoring all faults, is not just a trivial by-product, but something that serves to encourage dangerous misunderstandings. Japan now needs to know the West in much greater detail – just as it is, with all its faults, ugliness, selfishness and irrationality. In order to compete successfully, and also in order to avoid useless misunderstandings and unnecessary friction, we must begin to study the West anew, from a different angle, and with new objectives.

I have contended that Japan, as an 'information-deprived superpower', is stuck in a condition which is not only inimical to its own best interests, but one which makes it a problem for surrounding nations and the rest of the world as well. In the light of the remarks I have just made, it becomes apparent that there are two sides to this problem: first, the dearth of information and knowledge about Asia, which follows from ignorance and a lack of serious interest on the Japanese side; and second, a lack of the kind of information about Western nations that Japan needs in order to stand up to and compete with them. The solution to both aspects of this problem hangs on the question of whether the Japanese can awaken themselves from their century-long occidental dream and take a more relativistic, realistic view of the West – whether, in other words, Japan can break free from its Western-centred world view.

A comparative study of the economic and political developments in Japan and Thailand between 1868 and 1912

SOMMAI HOONTRAKOOL

I should like to begin by telling you why I decided to give a lecture on the economic and political developments in Japan and Thailand between 1868 and 1912. In my opinion, much of present-day Japan and Thailand have as their foundations the legacy of two reforms in the nineteenth century – the Meiji Restoration and the Chakkri Reformation.

I believe it would not be an exaggeration to say that the marvellous economic progress which Japan has achieved during the past fifty years was due, in large part, to the reforms made during the Meiji era. The foundations of democracy in Japan were also laid during this period. By the same token, Thailand, although far behind Japan in the development of her economy, also owes much to the reforms of this period for the growth rates which have been achieved and maintained over the past twenty years.

The successful transformations of both Japan and Thailand into modern states were, to a great extent, due to the determination and farsightedness of small groups of men. And among the men who contributed to the modernization of Japan was Fukuzawa Yukichi. His conviction in the value of Western education resulted in the founding of Keio University, which has served, and continues to serve, as an important seat of learning. Throughout its history, the University has provided government and industry with an abundant supply of able graduates.

Fukuzawa was also responsible for some of the reforms that were implemented during the Meiji era; for instance, he translated English textbooks on Western police systems, which helped the authorities in the setting up of a modern police force.

In view of this historical link, it seems fitting on this auspicious occasion that I speak about the Meiji period. Why then did I choose to undertake a comparative study? There are two reasons for this.

First, it has been argued that Thailand had a number of characteristics during this period which warrant a comparison with Japan. These common features fall into three categories: (1) historical similarities between Thailand and Japan; (2) the impetus for modernization in the two contemporary reigns of King Chulalongkorn and Emperor Meiji; and (3) other characteristics shared by the two countries, such as cultural homogeneity and the awareness of national identity.

Through a comparative study of King Chulalongkorn's Thailand and Emperor Meiji's Japan, the areas where the two countries differed and the variables which accounted for the contrasting degrees of success will emerge. Without comparison, the differences, similarities, causes and effects cannot be observed or inferred. By recognizing the differences which existed in the past, it will be possible to learn about some of the obstacles to the development of Thailand's economy.

Secondly, a comparative study provides the Japanese people with a more vivid picture of Thailand in this period, since much of what will be said about Thailand will be contrasted with developments in Japan.

In this paper I should also like to examine briefly the roles of King Chulalongkorn and Emperor Meiji in the modernization of their respective countries. There is no doubt that both monarchs' contributions were immense. At this point, I should like to read the tribute to Emperor Meiji by the British Prime Minister, Mr Asquith, which was published in *The Times* of London on 1 August 1912:

[The Emperor Meiji] representative of the most ancient dynasty of the world, whose annals go back 2,000 years, experienced during the years which passed since he succeeded his father a series of changes for which it would be difficult to find a parallel both in status of a Sovereign and the development of a people... He witnessed in less than 50 years his own transformation from a semi-divine, carefully sequestered figure, in the background of a national life, into a constitutional monarch, who, without losing any of the attributes of his ancestral position, became the mainspring, the central force, the pioneer, and the leader of a transformation at least as vital and as complete in every department of activity, political, social, industrial, intellectual, and moral, of his inherited dominion. Under his rule ... Japan has emerged from a seclusion which seemed inaccessible and beyond the reach of chance or change into the forefront of the family of nations.

In this respect, although King Chulalongkorn was not as highly regarded by leaders of foreign nations, the Thai people's respect for him was no less than the respect accorded to Emperor Meiji by the Japanese people, and his influence no less profound than that of Emperor Meiji.

It is an interesting historical coincidence that there emerged in the middle of the nineteenth century two contemporary reigns in Thailand and Japan of almost equal tenure. In Japan, Emperor Mutsuhito (Meiji) ascended to the throne in 1867 and reigned until his death in 1912, while in Thailand King Chulalongkorn (Rama V) ascended to the throne in 1868 and reigned until his death in 1910. Both monarchs came to the throne when they were still minors; regents were appointed to carry out official duties. At that time Japan and Thailand shared a number of characteristics in common. For example, while other countries in Asia had already been subject to colonization, Japan and Thailand were able to maintain their political independence. Also, both countries had a strong sense of national identity and cultural homogeneity. And both had a long tradition of selective cultural borrowing, often from the same source. Thus some aspects of Japanese culture were and are very similar to Thailand's own culture. The religion of both countries was Buddhism, which came direct from India in the case of Thailand and indirectly via China in the case of Japan. Moreover, rice was the major crop grown in Thailand as well as in Japan, and it formed the staple diet in both countries.

It should be pointed out, however, that although many elements in both countries' cultures were imported from other civilizations, since these were absorbed and transformed, they took on forms which were distinctly different from the originals.

Another similarity which both Thailand and Japan share is the fact that a few years before Emperor Meiji ascended to the throne, both countries, emerging from a long period of isolation, once again permitted foreigners to enter without restrictions. Furthermore, when faced with the threat of colonialism in the nineteenth century both countries resolved to modernize in order to avoid falling prey to it. The two countries were realistic about the intentions and power of foreigners. Both countries had to modernize by adapting to Western ways in such areas as administration, economic policy, infrastructure and customs. They had to appear 'civilized' in order to be accepted and to ward off excuses which might be made by the Western powers to step in and 'civilize' them. Reforms were carried out in the educational, administrative, legal, economic and social systems. Thailand and Japan were thus able to maintain their sovereignty throughout the period.

Interestingly, both Japan and Thailand carried out a number of reforms which were of a similar nature. For example, the most fundamental reforms which were launched in this period were the abolition of diarchy in Japan and the emancipation of slaves in Thailand. In the early part of Emperor Meiji's reign, the rank or caste of 'samurai' was abolished; the samurai were thus swept up into the masses. Old privileges were abolished, and all lines of promotion were open to the people. Likewise, in Thailand the abolition of slavery lifted a large proportion of the population to the rank of free citizens. The nobles, whose wealth had been determined partly by the number of slaves in their possession, lost much of their old status and privileges.

Apart from this, both Japan and Thailand undertook similar reforms to bring about a strong, centralized state. Both countries revised their legal and social systems in accordance with Western practices. Furthermore, both sought to modernize their respective armies.

Despite the fact that a number of similar reforms were launched in Thailand and Japan, even before the end of the nineteenth century a disparity could be observed in the results of those modernization efforts designed to develop the economy and national power.

This period saw a highly successful economic development in Japan. Progress was made in the agricultural as well as in the industrial sector. Between 1878 and 1882, through improvements in methods and techniques, substantial increases in agricultural production were realized in Japan. The rise in land productivity has been estimated at 80 per cent, while labour productivity is estimated to have risen by 140 per cent. At the same time, light and small-scale industries also expanded rapidly, particularly those involved in the production of textiles. Moderate success was also achieved in the medium- and large-scale industries.

Thailand, on the other hand, made no such progress. Although there was a significant increase in rice production, this stemmed from such factors as an increase in the labour force for rice-growing and the replacement of other crops with rice. However, there was no change in the methods and techniques of production, and consequently there was no increase in the productivity of the work-force or in that of the land. As for the industrial sector, no significant progress was observed during this period. In fact, there was a decline in the output of Thai manufactured goods; although records show some increase in the tin and teak industries, these were operated by foreigners and did not contribute to the development of the economy.

The contrast between Japan and Thailand in the results of their modernization programmes can also be seen in the national power and international status of the two countries.

Towards the end of the nineteenth century, Japan's status had been elevated to a level equivalent to that of a Western country. In 1902, Japan made an alliance with Great Britain, and this was followed by treaties with other Western powers. This was the first time in modern history for an Asian country to become an ally of a Western power.

In contrast to Japan, Thailand in the late nineteenth century was still struggling to maintain political independence. Caught between the French and the British spheres of influence, Thailand became a pawn in the rivalry of two powers. In order to preserve her independence, Thailand had to concede a sizeable part of her territories to the Western powers. However, when you consider that Britain had taken control of Burma and Malaysia, while France had colonized Indo–China, the loss of some territories was but a small price to pay. It was only in 1904 that agreements between France and Great Britain finally guaranteed Thailand her independence. Thus, unlike Japan, which looked outward to secure a place in the club of world powers, Thailand was preoccupied with a defensive policy of diplomatic manoeuvring for her survival.

Why then was Japan so successful in her modernization programmes, while Thailand achieved only limited success with her own programmes? In my opinion, there were many factors which contributed to this disparity. First, the levels of development of the two countries during that period were not the same. There were differences in the prevailing conditions as well as in the infrastructure – by these I mean the literacy rate, the size of the population, and the political as well as the commercial structure. Secondly, some of the reforms which were launched in Thailand and Japan, although similar in nature, had vastly differing effects. Thirdly, a number of reforms which were implemented in Japan had no counterpart in Thailand; these contributed greatly to the development of the country.

In order to give some idea of the advantages which Japan had over Thailand in terms of development, I shall now point out some of the basic differences which existed in the prevailing conditions and infrastructures of our two countries at that time.

To begin with, there were vast differences between Japan and Thailand in the standard and level of education. When Emperor Meiji ascended to the throne, there were already many *han* schools established throughout the country to teach the children of samurai families the cultural, moral and martial subjects necessary for their duties. Besides these, there were also over twenty thousand temple schools, or *terakoya*, which had been set up throughout Japan to teach reading, writing and arithmetic to the farmers and townspeople who needed such skills in their daily lives. Moreover, a few high schools and institutes had already been established during the late Tokugawa period.

Thailand, on the other hand, had only a few schools and no institutes for higher education. The schools were mainly located in the capital, with the result that a very large proportion of the population was unable to receive a proper education.

There were also significant differences between the two countries in the areas of commerce and finance. There was virtually no commercial class in Thailand until the influx of the Chinese during the reigns of Rama V (King Chulalongkorn) and Rama VI; this is in sharp contrast to Japan, where the growth of a native commercial class can be traced back to the Tokugawa period. Furthermore, the authorities in Thailand enjoyed a monopoly in major areas of commerce and industry which, together with the exploitation of the pariah class, served to inhibit economic development. Commerce itself was far more developed in Japan than in Thailand; for instance, the large trading houses already existed during the Tokugawa period.

A relatively comprehensive monetary system had already existed in Japan even before Emperor Meiji ascended to the throne. There were many exchange houses and local forms of money, which greatly facilitated market transactions. This was not the case with Thailand.

The local market in Japan was far larger than that in Thailand. At the beginning of Emperor Meiji's reign the population of Japan is estimated to have been thirty million; towards the end of his reign this had reached approximately sixty million. During the same period, the population of Thailand is estimated to have grown from four million to six million. Thus there were many more potential customers in Japan than in Thailand for the products which would be put on the market as a result of the setting up of new industries. As a result, many projects which were feasible for Japan were not feasible for Thailand. The concentration of the population in places like Tokyo, Kyoto and Osaka gave Japan a further advantage: an organized central market.

Towards the end of the Tokugawa period, farming methods were fairly well developed in Japan, as were weaving skills and other handicrafts. The transport system was also better organized in Japan than in Thailand. Land and sea routes were extensive enough to support nationwide commodity markets centred on rice but also encompassing other goods.

It should be noted too that, although both countries had once allowed foreigners to conduct trade with them, the effects of these activities on their respective economies were very different. With the start of foreign commerce, the traditional distribution system in Japan fell into chaos, and the commercial and industrial guilds were destroyed. Although exports of silk thread, tea and other commodities promoted the development of rural industries, they also caused the breakdown of the self-sufficient, rural-based economy. Thus Japan's economy was ready to accept a new system – the capitalist system.

In Thailand, the re-emergence of foreign trade left the old system untouched. Thailand's economy remained self-sufficient and rural-based. This was due in part to the fact that foreign traders were not as interested in the commodities which Thailand had to offer as they were in those which Japan was able to offer. It was also partly due to the King's monopoly over the commodities.

There were also differences in the type of leaders which both countries had, and in the political situations in which they found themselves. In the case of Japan, the leadership consisted of experienced samurai, while in Thailand the leaders were mostly young princes. But of more significance is the fact that Japan's leaders were more secure in their power; they were comparatively free from domestic challenge and international pressures, whereas Thailand's leaders were insecure. On the domestic scene, the young leaders of Thailand encountered the opposition of their predecessors. They were not able to secure their position until later, but by then they were faced with increasing international threats.

In this connection, it may be said that the foundation of Japan's development into a modern nation was to a large extent laid during the peaceful years of isolation in the feudal Tokugawa period. Apart from anything else, the experience gained by the ruling warrior class during that period accounted for the presence of men capable of running the new bureaucratic government and its institutions in the Meiji period.

Owing to the differences so far mentioned, Japan was in a much better position to modernize her country than was Thailand, which partly explains the differences in the results of the modernization programmes of the two countries. At the same time, I believe that the reforms which Japan alone undertook, combined with the differing impact of common reforms which both countries launched, were also responsible for the development gap between the two countries.

I turn now to consider some of the reforms which were

implemented – but did not have the same impact – in both countries.

The abolition of slavery in Thailand and the abolition of diarchy in Japan represent good examples of this phenomenon. In terms of political implications, the two reforms can be considered to be of equal importance. A sizeable proportion of each country's population was granted full citizenship, giving them opportunities that had never existed before. Previously there had been a nation within a nation; authority was divided, so the old and the strong had enjoyed all the privileges. But with these old privileges abolished, all lines of promotion were open to the people.

Nonetheless, the economic effects of these two reforms were very different. In Japan, as a result of the reform, the samurai voluntarily surrendered their hereditary incomes and were given a sum equivalent to six years' worth of their salaries, while those having life incomes received a lump sum equal to four years' pay. By this means a large number of non-producers became productive, the finances of the state were relieved and national wealth naturally increased. In addition, members of the pariah class, who had previously been exempted from taxes, were now treated like other citizens; thus the government was also able to find new sources of income.

For Thailand, the abolition of slavery did not have such a pronounced effect. The nobles, whose financial status was partly determined by the number of slaves in their possession, lost some of their 'wealth'. However, their need to work was not the same as that of the samurai; many of them owned land and were able to live off the rent. Thus the class of people who were non-producers prior to the reform remained non-productive.

Educational reform was also undertaken by both countries, but again the effects were very different. This was due, in large part, to differences in the extent of the reforms which were launched by the two countries.

Thai education was mainly confined to the palace and the monasteries. As a result, education in Thailand was associated with the dominant institutions and ideology, and was thus not conducive to fundamental change. Moreover, the types of education that were provided during this period were limited to the elementary level and were available only to members of the royal family and aristocrats; there were no high schools or institutes of higher education. Nor were there many foreign teachers in Thailand at this time.

Japan, on the other hand, established a public school system in the same mould as the systems of France and the United States. Development of human resources was promoted not only through the establishment of schools but also through efforts aimed at increasing enrolment. Moreover, many Japanese students received their education and training abroad, while only a few Thai students were sent overseas. Of those who went abroad, most were members of the royal family, a position which meant that there were no economic incentives for them to work hard. There were also many foreign experts (*yatoi*) in Japan. These foreigners set an example in industry – especially in mechanical pursuits, engineering and industrial exploitation – as well as in teaching and clerical work.

As a result of educational reform and the presence of foreign experts, the supply of skilled labour was greatly increased, which meant that the demand for labour in existing industries was met at a relatively low cost. Moreover, new industries that were being set up at the time had no need to worry about the problem of finding a sufficient supply of skilled workers. Besides this, an educated population meant that potential demand for new products rose together with actual demand.

During this period, modern transport and communication systems were set up in Thailand as well as in Japan. However, owing to the small size and low concentration of the population, these reforms were not as vigorously carried out in Thailand as they were in Japan; not did Thailand benefit from these modernization programmes to the same extent as Japan. Modern transportation systems enabled the already developed commercial centres of Osaka and Kyoto to send products to Tokyo and other cities more cheaply and conveniently than in the past. The new communication system – the telegraph service – enabled the many commercial centres around the country to receive news of the market very quickly. As a result, the demand for certain goods in one city was speedily matched by the supply of such goods from another city.

Other reforms that were launched by both countries were legal, administrative, and social in nature. Both countries introduced new legal systems in order to make them more comprehensive and just, and to appease the Western powers. Japan studied the French legal system, which it later adopted, while Thailand studied a number of systems – English, American, and French – adopting some aspects of a law from one system and copying other parts from another system.

It was also in this period that the new administrative system was established. Government ministries were set up to facilitate administration, and officers were recruited from a wider pool than before. The two governments were able to obtain capable men to fill the various posts.

Social reforms were also introduced in both countries. During the Tokugawa period, surnames had already been used in Japan, but they were only given to people from samurai families. The rest of the population had none. It was only in the Meiji period that everyone had a surname. Likewise in Thailand, surnames were introduced to the people around this time. Western-style dresses began to appear in Japan and in Thailand during this period, and other aspects of Western culture were also introduced. Although these reforms were important for the modernization of the social system, they contributed very little to the economic development of the country.

Another important factor which further widened the development gap between the two countries was the series of reforms that were carried out in Japan but which had no counterpart in Thailand.

As mentioned earlier, a monetary system had existed in Japan prior to the Meiji era; however, there was no national standard for coinage and currency. Over eleven hundred varieties of local paper issue were in circulation, which meant that trade was restricted as a transaction would only take place if the buyer could find a seller who would accept the type of paper money he had to offer. In order to solve this problem, and in order to create a new source of income for the government, officials were sent to the United States to study the mechanism of money; and on 4 April 1871 the new National Mint at Osaka was opened. The fact that there was a common currency further improved trading conditions in all regions. Apart from the issuance of a national currency, the authorities also brought out government convertible notes. Moreover, the government introduced a new financial system, based on the British system, in order to aid and control the development of financial institutions.

In Thailand, banknotes were introduced for the first time in 1889, when the Hong Kong and Shanghai Bank began to issue them. However, it was not until 1901 that the Thai government began to issue notes.

In Japan, in the private sector, as a result of encouragement from the government, the first commercial bank – Daiichi Kokuritsu Bank – was established in 1873, and the first private bank – The Mitsui Bank – appeared in 1876. Towards the end of Emperor Meiji's reign, well over twenty banks had been established. The setting up of these banks stimulated the mobilization of resources at the same time as providing the public and private sectors with new loan sources.

As far as Thailand was concerned, although foreign banks had opened branches in Bangkok as early as 1888, the first Thai bank – Siam Commercial Bank – was not founded until 1907.

There were also political reforms which played an important role in the development of Japan, reforms which had no equivalent in Thailand.

The first of these political reforms was the restoration of the emperor's power. By this I mean the transfer of power from the feudal lords back to the emperor. Implicit in this transfer of power was the transfer of wealth. Land which for centuries had been in the possession of private owners was successfully 'nationalized', and since the national income was mainly derived from tax on land, this transfer of wealth raised the government's income. One-tenth of the revenue raised in each prefecture was set apart as the governor's salary. After defraying expenses, the remainder went into the Imperial Treasury. The government also reserved to itself the appointment of all offices previously held under the feudal lords, which meant that it could select the best people for the jobs.

Secondly, Japan's written constitution of 1889 and the abolition of class distinctions had given the people incentives to work hard for themselves as well as for their country. Positions in the government and the armed forces were no longer restricted to a specific class. Thus, while Japan's political activity was characterized by great socio-political efficiency and a diversity of interests, Thai political activity was still limited to the narrow strata of legitimate participants. The majority of Thai people were non-political and belonged to no politically relevant groupings. This was due mainly to the relatively small population, which was scattered all over the country. As a result, political efficiency was minimal and change in the political and administrative apparatus could – and did – occur only when it served the interests of the political elites.

Therefore, it may be said that although Thailand and Japan shared many common characteristics, they were at different stages of development when they decided to launch their modernization programmes. The programmes themselves produced different results, and in some cases differed in nature as well as in form. Thus it was difficult for Thailand to emulate Japan's performance, even though radical changes did take place.

Finally, I should like to conclude with a brief examination of the roles played by King Chulalongkorn and Emperor Meiji in the modernization of their respective countries.

It is always difficult to measure a person's contribution to the development of society, but I think it can fairly be said that the contributions which King Chulalongkorn and Emperor Meiji made towards the modernization of their countries were immense.

Both monarchs came to the throne when they were very young; nevertheless, King Chulalongkorn and Emperor Meiji were called upon almost continually to play an active part in ruling their countries. On reaching adulthood they both became the most industrious of sovereigns. It was this strenuous activity that early on qualified them to gauge quickly the value and capacity of a man, and to read his motives. Thus it is not surprising that both rulers were surrounded by able men and wise counsellors.

The influence which both monarchs had over the reforms can be understood from their positions of power. Notwithstanding the constitution of 1889, Emperor Meiji had total control over all the major issues. If he had decided on a certain course of action, then it would be extremely difficult for anyone in Japan to oppose it. Likewise King Chulalongkorn, who was an absolute monarch, had the final word on all issues involving the country. However, this is not to say that the two monarchs did not encounter any opposition in bringing about changes, for there was opposition, sometimes strong opposition. For example, the nobles in Thailand opposed the abolition of slavery and tried to stop the reform. In Japan, Emperor Meiji also faced opposition from some samurai and clan leaders with respect to the abolition of feudalism and, to a lesser degree, when he set up the system of imperial governors.

Thus reforms which had been launched in Thailand and in Japan were partly – or in some cases mainly – due to the far-sightedness of the two monarchs. It is true that some of the reforms implemented were the result of foreign influence, and to some extent were designed to preserve the status of the monarch. But many other reforms were undertaken in order to modernize their respective countries so as to improve the welfare of their citizens.

Both rulers rose to every fresh occasion and met new demands and duties with cheerful regularity. They both realized the mystic influence of their positions, and used it wisely to further the development of their nations. It was by their example that the people of both countries began to accept the culture of the West, as well as its political and social systems. Through all the vicissitudes of their reigns, the two monarchs fulfilled their duties splendidly. They were always able to inspire enthusiasm in their subjects, to spur them on to worthy achievements.

However, it must be said that Emperor Meiji was faced with more problems than King Chulalongkorn, as his duties were far more burdensome than those of the Thai king. Emperor Meiji had to guide the ship of state between the radicals, who would plunge headlong into modern civilization and adopt everything foreign at once, and the conservatives, who would make changes only under compulsion. The Emperor was called upon to lead the nation in its effort to modernize. He renounced his old secluded life and entered upon the career that modern conditions required, so that the rest of the nation would follow his example. This he did gladly and without hesitation. He made many sacrifices for the sake of Japan. For example, during the time of the fourth parliament, when the making of economies in government expenditure and generally reducing official salaries were topics under intense discussion, the Emperor asked why there was nothing said about curtailing the expenses of the imperial household. Characteristically, Emperor Meiji declared that the palace expenditure must be cut first, then the others could follow.

Central banking in a developing country – the Philippine experience

ESCOLASTICA B. BINCE

Introduction

The Central Bank of the Philippines was created under its original charter, Republic Act No. 265 (1948), which provided the general objectives: maintenance of monetary stability; preservation of the international value and convertibility of the peso into other freely convertible currencies; and promotion of a rising level of production, employment and real income.

Presidential Decree No. 72, issued in 1972 upon the recommendation of the Joint IMF–CBP Banking Survey Commission, amended the Central Bank Charter and redefined its goals as follows:

(a) Primarily to maintain internal and external monetary stability in the Philippines and to preserve the international value of the peso and its convertibility into other freely convertible currencies.

(b) To foster monetary, credit and exchange conditions conducive to a balanced and sustainable growth of the economy.

Thus, like all central banks of recent vintage, the Central Bank of the Philippines has been given a role beyond the traditionally accepted function of merely maintaining the internal and external stability of the currency, by requiring it to provide the proper financial climate conducive to a continuous growth of the economy. While maintaining its independence from the fiscal authorities, its activities must be co-ordinated with other government agencies, thus sharing the responsibility of attaining a maximum rate of growth with stability.

The traditional function of a central bank is the maintenance of the domestic and external stability of the currency. The former is measured by the price indices which indicate the volume of goods and services a unit of money can purchase, while the latter is gauged by the exchange rate of one unit of the foreign currency commonly used in the settlement of international transactions. Though closely related, neither of these two values can be sacrificed for the sake of the other.

Formerly, the definition of monetary stability was limited to domestic and external stability, but since the Second World War this has been expanded to include full employment and economic growth. In fact, in some developing countries the emphasis is on rapid long-term economic growth, rather than on short-term achievement of full employment.

All central banks make use of traditional monetary instruments, but each adopts whatever technique or approach is suitable for its own economy and financial structure. In First World countries with well-developed financial structures, central banks can effectively make use of such instruments as reserve requirements, rediscounting and open market operations. However, in developing countries with varying economic levels and financial systems in the early stage of development, these instruments cannot readily be applied. By necessity, the main attention of central banks in these countries must be directed towards the development of the financial system, the inculcation of the banking habit, and the mobilization of financial resources.

Developing the financial structure

The evolution of the Philippine financial system has been influenced both by market forces and by a conscious government policy to build a financial structure responsive to the needs of a developing economy. The government has taken an innovative and flexible stance, and has made use of the valuable lessons learned from its own experience as well as those of other countries going through a similar process. It has also invited experts from other countries and international agencies for the purpose of obtaining an objective evaluation of its programmes and policies.

When the Central Bank started operating in 1949, the financial system was composed of only 13 institutions. By 1983, the financial network had expanded to a total of 1,132 institutions.

COMMERCIAL BANKS

Commercial banks, which started operating during the Spanish era, represent the largest single group within the country's financial system. They operate on a branch-banking organizational structure, with head offices in Metropolitan Manila. They offer all types of banking and other allied services so that they may be considered department stores of finance.

RURAL BANKS

In 1952, the need to provide an appropriate credit system capable of meeting the requirements of the common man gave rise to the Rural Bank Act (Republic Act No. 720). The essential features of the programme aimed at providing incentives to the organizers are: (i) Counterpart Capital Assistance from the government; (ii) exclusion of the government from active management by limiting its holdings to non-voting shares of preferred stock; (iii) provision of technical assistance, particularly in the organization stage; (iv) a training programme for rural banks' personnel; (v) farm advisory servicing for the supervised credit programmes; (vi) tax exemption privileges for rural banks with net assets not exceeding ₱1 million, with proportional exemption for banks with assets of up to ₱3 million; (vii) free notarization and registration of loan documents involving not more than ₱10,000; (viii) exemption from the publication requirement in case of foreclosure proceedings where loan principal plus interest does not exceed ₱20,000; and (ix) rediscounting at subsidized rates.

THRIFT BANKS

Thrift banks – which include savings and mortgage banks, private development banks and stock savings banks – were organized primarily to draw funds from household and individual savers, and to invest such funds in loans secured by bonds, real estate mortgages and other forms of security. The main objective of thrift banks is to encourage home building.

Republic Act (RA) No. 3779, the law governing the organization and operation of savings and loan associations, was promulgated on 22 June 1963. The law laid down minimum requirements for their establishment and the protection of the public. 'Savings and loan associations' are of two types. Non-stock savings and loan associations are engaged in accumulating the savings of their members and, using such accumulation, in granting loans to their members. Stock savings and loan associations, aside from performing similar functions, also invest the accumulated savings together with their capital in productive enterprises or government securities.

Private development banks were created by virtue of RA No. 4093 on 19 June 1964. These banks assumed all the obligations of savings and mortgage banks as provided in the General Banking Act. The primary objective was to promote agriculture and industry, and place medium- and long-term credit within easy reach of people at reasonable cost. A private development bank is organized in the form of a stock corporation owned by citizens of the Philippines. However, upon the representation of its stockholders, the Development Bank of the Philippines may subscribe to additional capital stock.

SPECIALIZED GOVERNMENT BANKS

Specialized government banks play special roles in the economic development of the country. The Rehabilitation Finance Corporation was established by RA No. 85 on 26 October 1946, mainly to provide long-term industrial and agricultural credits. Subsequently, on 14 June 1958, RA No. 2081 converted it into the Development Bank of the Philippines.

The Land Bank of the Philippines was created by RA No. 3844 on 22 June 1963, to serve as the implementing instrument of the Land Reform Program of the country.

The Philippine Amanah Bank, authorized by Presidential Decree No. 264 on 2 August 1973, has the primary objective of providing banking facilities to the Muslim population of Mindanao and Palawan.

OFFSHORE BANKING

The most significant innovation introduced in the development of the banking system was the establishment of Offshore Banking Units (OBUs) through the issuance of Presidential Decree No. 1034 on 30 September 1976.

Earlier, a foreign currency deposit system (FCDS), which was the forerunner of offshore banking, was instituted within the domestic banking system. Both were expected to coexist, each with a clear delineation of the area of primary activity. The FCDS was to continue its role of attracting foreign currency deposits, while the OBUs would make possible the transformation of Manila into a regional financial centre which would provide funds for Philippine and regional enterprises. The former was expected to generate short-term funds; the latter, long- and medium-term resources.

The Manila offshore banking model also took into consideration the existence of established offshore centres in the region – such as Singapore, Hong Kong and Tokyo. However, it would not compete with them, but rather complement them in expanding transactions with other parts of the world, especially the Middle East countries.

Offshore banking units, which are branches, subsidiaries or affiliates of foreign banking corporations, are authorized to conduct banking transactions in foreign currencies through the receipt of funds principally from external sources, and the utilization of such funds for undertakings inside or outside the country. Under the system, foreign currencies accepted and held by OBUs in the course of their business are considered 'deposits'. The Central Bank of the Philippines supervises the operation and activities of these units. However, in line with the country's free enterprise policy, the Central Bank only sees to it that foreign exchange regulations are not circumvented.

On 18 March 1977, the Central Bank approved the application of eleven foreign banks to operate offshore banks in the country.

Initially, offshore banks were authorized to engage only in external transactions, but were subsequently allowed to conduct limited domestic transactions. For example, an OBU may open a letter of credit for the importation of machinery by residents who are recipients of OBU long-term loans approved by the Central Bank.

NON-BANK FINANCIAL INTERMEDIARIES

A new emerging force in financial intermediation are the so-called non-bank financial intermediaries; this term refers to all other types of financial institutions which make use of alternative methods of mobilizing funds other than regular deposits. Included in this group are specialized government institutions like the Social Security System, the Government Service Insurance System and, before it was absorbed by the Land Bank of the Philippines in 1982, the Agricultural Credit Administration, as well as private institutions like investment houses, investment companies, finance companies, insurance companies, pawnshops, credit unions, and building and loan associations. These institutions, which are organized under their own enabling statutes, are officially grouped under Presidential Decree No. 71, which amended the General Banking Act.

In June 1983 the non-bank financial intermediaries numbered 1,141 institutions; among these were 53 investment houses, 341 financing companies, and 105 securities dealers.

Banking reforms

Over a period of time, the needs of the economy acquire additional dimensions which frequently are not just economic but also social, the reconciliation of which often poses difficult problems. Developments, both domestic and external, gave rise to the banking reforms of 1972 and 1980, which had the same basic objective of evolving a financial system responsive to the needs of a developing economy.

With the accumulation of legislative measures creating different types of financial institutions, the banking system had become unusually complicated and over-fragmented. The rise of new forms of financial intermediation, especially the so-called money markets, also challenged the effectiveness of the Central Bank in allocating financial resources.

As a consequence, the Joint IMF–CBP Banking Survey Commission was constituted in 1971 to conduct an overall revision of the financial system. The findings of the Commission formed the basis of the 1972 reforms. The Commission made the following recommendations, which were reflected in subsequent amendments to the Central Bank Act and the General Banking Act in 1972 and 1973:

(a) The addition of more commercial banks was to be discouraged; branch banking was to be preferred over unit banking.

(b) Monetary and fiscal measures were to be applied uniformly for institutions performing similar services or enjoying similar benefits.

(c) The Central Bank was given authority and responsibility not only over the monetary system (banks) but over the entire financial and credit system. For the first time, the Central Bank was granted regulatory powers over non-banking units.

(d) The responsibility of the Central Bank was redefined primarily as the maintenance of monetary stability, while the responsibility for promoting growth was to be shared with the planning agencies of the government. This redefinition of responsibilities called for a reorganization of the Monetary Board to include the Minister of Planning and the Chairman of the Board of Industries in place of the President of the Philippine National Bank and the Chairman of the Development Bank of the Philippines.

(e) The Central Bank was given more flexibility in exercising its powers consistent with the maintenance of monetary stability.

The reforms of 1980 were indicated by the report of a Joint IMF–World Bank Mission to the Philippines in 1979. The Mission was particularly concerned with the need to increase the flow of savings in the financial system and to encourage an increasing proportion of such flows to borrowers on a medium- and longer-term basis. For this purpose, the Mission suggested the development of an active capital market and the lender-of-last-resort facility of the Central Bank to meet the liquidity requirements of financial institutions.

Mr Ernesto Fernandez Hurtado, former Director-General of the Banco de Mexico, was also invited to review the financial system under the same terms of reference as the IMF–World Bank Mission. Like the Mission, Mr Hurtado attributed the then prevailing preference for short-term credit to excessive specialization in the system.

However, unlike the Mission, Mr Hurtado urged the conversion of commercial banks into large and strong multi-purpose banks which could be used to mobilize savings and direct funds to long-term credits through their ability to offer financial instruments in varying forms, sizes and returns which would meet the requirements of the saving public. With their substantial capital, these banks could operate as well in development credit and financing.

The 1980 reforms as embodied in Batas Pambansa Nos. 61–67, dated 1 April 1980, had two primary objectives: (i) increasing competitive conditions for greater efficiency, and (ii) increasing the availability of and access to long-term funds. The first objective was to be attained by eliminating enforced 'legal specializations' under the basic principle of 'a bank can do what any other bank can do'. However, because of certain peculiar limitations inherent in the country, it was felt that the full adoption of what is generally known as 'universal banking' was not desirable. Instead, it was decided that for the present, a modified version in the form of a more competitive banking system based on universal banking concepts, known as 'expanded commercial banking', could be introduced.

Another technique for expanding competition was to broaden the range of services a bank could offer, such as underwriting, securities dealing and equity investments; this resulted in economies of scale.

The economic development process in the Philippines has often been hampered by the lack of long-term funds, both for debt and equity needs. Most often, industries finance their equity and long-term requirements with short-term funds. If, for one reason or another, the climate for extending or renewing these loans becomes unfavourable, financial upheavals affecting the very foundation of the financial system occur. This situation emphasizes the need for long-term credit.

The policy of developing longer-term credit has sometimes been called 'term transformation'. Initially, although deposits are exclusively short-term, a portion remaining untouched for a relatively longer period may be used for long-term lending. Of course, there should be longer-term placements to match longer-term loans. The major objective, therefore, is to encourage long-term placements to finance equity and long-term loans. The first step is to make long-term placements more attractive. This could be done, for example, by including long-term payments as collateral for access to the discount window, or through preferential reserve requirements, or by completely exempting longer-term placements. These were accomplished through amendments to existing laws and certain administrative policies.

Monetary instruments

The Central Bank of the Philippines' charter provides it with certain instruments, such as the authority to change the reserve requirements, rediscount rates and portfolio ceilings or engage in open market operations and other activities for liquidity management. However, the need not only to control the amount of liquidity but also to allocate limited resources to promising sectors – particularly those engaged in the production of basic items such as food, clothing and shelter, as well as export goods for balance of payments purposes – has limited the use of such instruments and unorthodox techniques have often had to be resorted to.

Starting in December 1978, in conjunction with the negotiation of an Extended Fund Facility with the IMF, the Central Bank began operating a so-called monetary budget in order to monitor and control the expansion of net domestic assets within desirable limits consistent with the targeted GNP rate of growth and balance of payments. The monetary budget is determined by an allowable expansion of reserve assets which could be effectively controlled by the Central Bank through its discount window and open market operations.

REDISCOUNT OPERATIONS OF THE CENTRAL BANK

The Central Bank is authorized to grant rediscounts, loans and advances to banking institutions as a means of regulating the cost, availability and character of bank credit, and to provide the banking system with liquid funds in times of need. In other words, rediscounting plays a twofold role of directing credit to desired priority areas and providing liquidity to banks.

In the first thirty years of Central Bank operation, the discount window has been used mainly as an allocative instrument to support development goals. It has not only provided liquidity to banks with a view to encouraging them to extend loans for higher priority areas like agriculture; it has also permitted them to rediscount at preferential rates. This ensures an interest spread attractive enough to induce the flow of funds to preferred economic activities.

The 1980 financial reforms liberalized the discount window so as to include a lender-of-last-resort facility. This created a 'liquidity mechanism' open to banks and financial institutions with quasi-banking functions to prevent undue fluctuations in money market rates spawned by short-term fund deficiencies.

The pressures exerted by competing demands on the economy have posed serious problems in limiting the areas for preferential rates, which ideally should be temporary in nature. Recent developments point to the reduction of priority areas to a minimum, and eventually limiting access to the discount window to liquidity requirements at market-oriented rates.

OPEN MARKET OPERATIONS

As used in this paper, the term 'open market operations' refers to all Central Bank activities aimed at accomplishing its reserve money objectives, including the buying and selling of government securities, but excluding changes in reserve requirements and rediscount rates.

In the early years of central banking, operations in the open market were limited to the purchase and sale of government securities with extremely low interest rates, very much below market rates, and therefore they were not actively traded. For lack of an organized market, they were bought only by banks and were mainly used to form part of their reserves against deposit liabilities. Subsequently, in the late sixties, the market was activated to help develop a long-term capital market, with the introduction of treasury bills by the National Government. These bills carried a comparatively higher rate of interest, with terms ranging from 69 to 182 days. By 1975, maturities from 35 to 364 days constituted the offerings. They were issued on a discount basis under competitive and non-competitive bidding and were payable at maturity date at par value.

In 1970, to promote further the twin objectives of improving open market instruments and developing the capital market, the Central Bank issued its own securities known as Central

Bank Certificates of Indebtedness (CBCIs) as a supplement to the available range of government securities.

The National Government has taken steps towards rationalizing the issue of securities by adopting the auction method in the sale of securities. Steps were also taken to align the yields of different government securities with market rates for the purpose of eventually establishing an active securities market. As part of the rationalization process, the CBCIs are being phased out and are being replaced by treasury bills.

INTEREST RATE POLICY

While most developed countries have always considered the discount rate as the most potent instrument for monetary management, developing countries like the Philippines have started to make use of it only in recent years. This is because decisions to borrow are basically influenced by the availability and ease of obtaining credit rather than the cost of money.

Interest rate policy in the Philippines can be traced to 1956 when the Central Bank started to regulate interest rates on bank deposits. Prior to 1956, the Central Bank did not formally regulate interest rates since the Anti-Usury Law – approved in 1916 and prescribing a 12-14 per cent ceiling on lendings – indirectly limited the interest rates on bank deposits. Interest rates on funds from informal sources were virtually free from any control due to the difficulty of implementing the law. The primary concern of the authorities was to protect the borrowers by preventing the imposition of unreasonable interest on loans. Interest rates on deposits were extremely low then compared to the allowable maximum lending rates, so that banks enjoyed a spread much wider than those in developed countries.

The period from 1956 to 1973 was characterized by rigid, low interest rates. Ceilings were prescribed on the interest that could be paid on all types of deposits. The interest allowed on time deposits was almost equal to that paid on savings deposits. Minimum adjustments on the original ceiling of 2 per cent were made in 1957, 1960, 1965, and finally in 1967 when a ceiling of 6 per cent was set. As an initial attempt to encourage longer-term placements, an interest rate differential was introduced in April 1969, setting the interest rate on savings at 6 per cent, 6.5 per cent for 90-day time deposits, and 7 per cent for 360-

day time deposits. This period was also characterized by an increasing gap between deposit and lending rates. This did not promote greater efficiency in the financial system as it provided a bias in the form of borrowings to finance investments rather than encouraging the business sector to raise its funds in an equity market.

The years 1974–80 were marked by frequent rate revisions, particularly on the deposit side, in order to make interest rates an active instrument in the mobilization of savings. Through the Monetary Board, the Central Bank was granted authority to prescribe and change the maximum rates of interest 'for loans or forbearance of money, goods, or credits whenever warranted by prevailing economic conditions but not more often than once every 12 months'. This was, in effect, an amendment to the Anti-Usury Law.

In early 1974, the Commission on Interest Rate Policy, an inter-agency group, was created to study the level and structure of interest rates, applicable laws, rules and regulations. On 15 July 1974, the Commission recommended a package of measures aimed at encouraging long-term funds from investment and at providing a more equitable return to savers. On the recommendation of the Commission, the interest rate ceiling was raised once more on time deposits of less than two years in an effort to align interest rates prevailing in the country with the rest of the world. The interest rate ceilings on deposits with maturities of more than two years were lifted. The 'legal rate of interest', defined as the interest paid on loans where no interest rate was stipulated, was also raised from 6 per cent to 12 per cent. In addition, attempts were made to stabilize and possibly lower money market rates to stem the inordinate flow of funds from regular bank deposits.

In 1977 another set of circulars was issued, further increasing the interest rate ceiling on savings and time deposits but reducing those paid for money market placements. Commensurately, a higher ceiling on interest paid for loans was instituted. In 1980, the extension of loans with maturities of one to four years with floating interest rates was allowed. The interest rates would be based on a market reference rate (MRR) computed on the basis of interest paid on time deposits with a maturity of over 730 days to be announced every 15 days. This signified the first attempt to have loans pay an interest rate dictated by the market as the MRR was not subject to any interest rate ceiling.

The financial reforms of 1980, instituted to encourage the emergence of bigger, more diversified and more competitive financial intermediaries, gave rise to the need for greater flexibility in the mobilization of resources, particularly long-term funds. A completely floating interest rate policy was instituted by a number of circulars dated 27 February 1981. The remaining ceilings on time deposits and deposit substitutes with maturities of less than two years were lifted. Likewise, ceilings on loans with maturities of more than two years but less than four years were removed. However, that on short-term instruments was retained, as an interim measure, to effect a smooth transition and enable it to serve as a bench-mark for interest rates with longer terms. As part of the deregulation measures, revisions were also made in the reserve requirements and the rediscounting mechanism. After the market had been established, the deregulation of interest rates was completed on 1 January 1983, with the lifting of the remaining ceilings on short-term loan transactions. Simultaneously, a prime rate monitoring scheme was instituted to provide the borrowing public with up-to-date information on the lowest lending rate charged by banks.

MANAGEMENT OF THE EXTERNAL VALUE OF THE PESO

The par value of the peso was defined in the Central Bank Charter: 'the gold value of the peso is seven and thirteen twenty-firsts (7-13/21) grains of gold, nine tenths (0.900) fine, which is equivalent to the United States dollar parity of the peso as provided in Sec. 6 of Commonwealth Act No. 699.' When the Central Bank started operations in 1949, the exchange rate of the peso to the dollar was ₱2 to US$1. Because of the close political and economic ties of the Philippines with the United States, Central Bank foreign exchange policy during the first decade of its operations was aimed at defending the par value of the peso and adhering very closely to the behaviour of the dollar in its relation with other currencies of the world. Almost all foreign exchange transactions were negotiated in US dollars and the bulk of the international reserves was held in the same currency.

In the latter part of 1949, the following currencies other than US dollars were made eligible to form part of the international reserves: (1) the pound sterling, (2) the Deutschmark, (3) the Swiss franc, and (4) the Canadian dollar. Additions to the list were made later so that there is now a total of twelve currencies that are eligible. The seven additional currencies are: (1) the Japanese yen, (2) the Hong Kong dollar, (3) the French franc, (4) the Dutch guilder, (5) the Austrian schilling, (6) the Belgian franc, and (7) the Singapore dollar.

Because of an expansion in foreign exchange transactions with some countries, their currencies are also acceptable for foreign exchange transactions but are not eligible as part of the international reserves. These currencies are (1) the Australian dollar, (2) the Bahraini dinar, (3) the Malaysian dollar, (4) the Saudi Arabian rial, and (5) the Italian lira.

During the first ten years of central banking, the country was involved in the rehabilitation and reconstruction of the economy, giving rise to heavy import bills to meet not only the requirements of rehabilitation but also to satisfy pent-up demand for consumer items. Heavy trade deficits were likewise incurred while export industries destroyed during the war years were being rehabilitated. Initially, heavy United States Government expenditures – which included war damage payments and veterans' backpay outlays – financed the trade deficit. But when these sources tapered off, the international reserves dropped to a dangerously low level, requiring drastic remedial measures in the form of controls. This was originally intended to be a stopgap measure, but exchange and trade restrictions remained in force for almost a decade. While controls brought along negative developments like black-marketing, graft and corruption, and over-protection of inefficient industries, they nevertheless spurred the beginning of industrialization in the form of industries engaged in the production of import substitutes. The share of the manufacturing sector in the Net Domestic Product (at factor cost) rose from 12.6 per cent in 1949 to 19 per cent in 1960 (1967 prices = 100).

Contrary to expectations, the establishment of light industries, most of which being merely assembling and repacking units, did not reduce the import bill. The import bill continued to rise as the demand for imported goods failed to decline; instead, a shift from finished consumer items to raw materials and semi-processed goods took place. Moreover, despite the 17 per cent exchange tax levied to close the gap between the official exchange rate and the black market rate, the external value of the peso continued to deteriorate, indicating a need for a change in strategy. A gradual decontrol programme was instituted on 25 April 1960, to shift the burden of controlling imports from monetary measures to the more effective use of fiscal instruments, particularly tariffs. Quantitative restrictions were to be phased out over a period of four years by releasing 25 per cent to the free market every year. Due to favourable initial results, decontrol was accelerated. Full decontrol was attained on 21 January 1962, less than two years after its adoption, except for the requirement to surrender 20 per cent of export receipts to the Central Bank at the official rate of exchange. In 1965, the peso was officially devalued for the first time to ₱3.90 – US$1, a rate almost equal to that prevailing in the free market since 1962.

Adverse external developments coupled with growing fiscal deficits caused serious balance of payments problems during the late sixties. One factor which contributed to the crisis was the heavy debt-servicing burden arising from the bunching-up of short-term loans used to finance the long-term requirements of industry. This required the adoption of a stabilization programme in 1970, a salient feature of which was the floating of the peso. The peso was cut off from the US dollar's apron-strings, its value being determined by the demand and supply factors in the foreign exchange market.

It was determined that the long-term solution to the perennial balance of payments problem lay in the expansion of exports and invisible receipts from tourism and Filipino workers abroad; the floating rate was intended to provide an incentive to boost receipts from these sources.

In conjunction with the stabilization programme, conscious external debt management was initiated with the dual objectives of promoting economic growth through the optimum utilization of external credits, and ensuring the maintenance of a debt structure compatible with the repaying capacity of the country. Two major constraints on Philippine borrowing have been effectively used as basic tools of debt management. RA No. 6142 limits the level of total debt service payments in any given year to 20 per cent of the total foreign exchange receipts in the preceding year. The other constraint is an annual ceiling on new external debt approvals, which is determined annually in consultation with the International Monetary Fund under a stand-by arrangement. Even in the absence of a stand-by arrangement, the Central Bank continues to observe a self-imposed ceiling. In pursuit of these debt management objectives, the strategy calls for a system of prior Central Bank approval of all loan proposals, both public and private. Approval of foreign loans is basically limited to the following areas: food production, power and energy exploration, export-oriented projects, and communication and transportation. The terms of all loans are also carefully monitored.

Promotional activities

Within the context of the 'climate' prevailing in developing countries, central banking has become more complicated, opening new horizons for its operations. Although they cannot properly be considered within the scope of central banking, activities that may contribute to the attainment of economic goals have been performed by central banks. The Central Bank of the Philippines is no exception: it has engaged in informative and educational campaigns to acquaint not only bankers but the general public as well with certain disciplines that tend to promote the national economy.

The most noteworthy of these campaigns were the National Savings for Progress Campaign, the Countryside Credit and Collection Campaign, and the Suwerte sa Bangko (Fortune in the Bank) Raffle.

The National Savings for Progress Campaign was a massive nationwide drive initiated by the Central Bank with the active participation of several government agencies and support of the private banking system. The purpose was to instil the general public with a savings consciousness and to teach the concept of responsible credit use.

The Countryside Credit and Collection Campaign was

launched to reduce the high rate of arrearages of farmer-borrowers from rural banks.

The Suwerte sa Bangko Raffle was an innovative project designed to make remittances through the banking system more financially rewarding and interesting to overseas workers and their beneficiaries. For every US$100 surrendered by an overseas worker or other individual to a local bank, a raffle ticket was issued which entitled the holder to win ₱100,000. Every month, ten raffle holders were declared winners.

Tourism continues to be an important aspect of the government development programme. The government's support for the tourist industry was manifested in the construction of international class hotels in the greater Manila area which were financed by government banks and financial institutions with financial support from the Central Bank.

The Central Bank of the Philippines was largely instrumental in the construction of the Philippine International Convention Centre which has been – and continues to be – the venue of many important international conventions and conferences.

Economic and financial relations with Japan

Japan plays a very important role in the balance of payments situation of the Philippines. It is one of the country's leading trading partners, running a close second to the United States in terms of total trade. The balance of trade has uniformly been in favour of Japan, although the trade gap has been narrower. The principal exports consist of copper concentrates, iron ore agglomerates, bananas (fresh), semiconductor devices, and nickel concentrates; the most important imports are canned sardines, polyethylene in primary forms, iron and steel coils for re-rolling, cold-rolled sheets and plates, and seamless iron or steel pipes and tubes.

Similarly, Japan leads all other countries in providing much-needed foreign exchange to finance the development requirements of both public and private sectors. It has provided commercial and concessional loans with long-term maturities of fifteen years and above, with interest rates below those prevailing in the capital market. Japan has also entered into some joint-

venture arrangements with nationals, particularly in the areas
of automotive assembly and steel (sintering plant).

Even in the area of aids and grants, Japan has been one of the
principal providers of both institutional and personal remittances. However, their impact can be greatly enhanced by a
change in direction and emphasis. The Philippines is endowed
with vast agricultural lands and is surrounded by extensive
coastlines. On the other hand, Japan, because of its limited
area, is unable to satisfy the increasing consumption requirements of its population internally. Technical and financial
assistance from Japan should be directed towards the production of agricultural products mutually beneficial to both countries. This has been started in the production of bananas and
prawns, but other similar areas could be explored. To provide
an incentive for industrialization, the primary processing of
such commodities, which can be performed cheaper in a
developing economy, should also be initiated. The comparative
advantage of the Philippines in the production of agricultural
commodities, as well as its proximity to Japan, will result in the
supply of better quality goods at lower cost. This in turn will be
translated into increased income for local farmers, enabling
them to purchase industrial items, of which Japan is a principal
supplier. Indirectly, this will contribute towards the success of
the countryside credit campaign, since the main reason for the
inability of the farmers to pay their obligations stems from low
and unstable incomes.

Conclusion

I have been to Japan several times in the past, most often to
negotiate loans with financial institutions. Normally discus-
sions were centered on interest rates, terms and conditions to be
observed, but these conferences gave me a rare opportunity to
see the other side of Japan – the side that is willing to learn, even
to the extent of accepting criticisms, in order to promote better
understanding among Asians. This emboldens me to call on
Japan to view Philippine financial developments with understanding and not to judge the measures we adopt in the light of
policies found effective by the more developed economies of the

world. After all, recent events have confirmed the long-held view that central banking is not an exact science. It is continuously going through changes because of developments not even dreamt of in the past.

I should like to close this paper by paraphrasing the view of central banking given by Jürg Niehans in the conclusion to his book, *The Theory of Money* (1978, p.294):

> Central banking is an art which is not likely to become a precise science however far monetary theory may progress. A central banker is a doer whose field of action is the ever-changing stream of economic events, where every day may pose new problems requiring new solutions. A central bank will use economic science as a commander of armies uses military science: it is useful and sometimes indispensable, but it can never provide a complete recipe for victory.

I think this view of central banking is very appropriate for a developing country like the Philippines.

China's policies for energy and technology, and economic relations with Japan

SUN SHANGQING

Introduction

China and Japan are the two major powers in Asia. Japan's territory is small and its natural resources cannot be called abundant, but it possesses a highly developed economy and advanced technology; it has therefore become an economic giant of global stature.

China, on the other hand, has an expansive territory, considerable natural resources, a large population and thus a large domestic market. However, the level of economic development is still low; it lags behind Japan in terms of science, technology, and administration.

Asia's position and role in the development of the world economy is receiving increasing attention. But with the spotlight thrown on it, the economy of Japan must begin to grope towards a new form of development, a development that will give it fresh impetus. And China, for its part, must begin to accelerate its economic development. It is desirable that both China and Japan strongly promote further economic exchanges, and that each establishes economic ties with other countries, both within and without Asia, based on the principles of equality and mutual prosperity. China and Japan enjoy a very special relationship – historically, geographically and culturally – and they should be able to establish an important precedent for economic co-operation between two nations with differing social systems and at differing stages of economic development.

At present, China is in the middle of actively promoting modernization and construction plans, implementing policies for opening the country and activating the domestic economy.

From now on it is determined to develop further its economic and technological ties with Japan, in the hope that the areas of co-operation will multiply. And I am convinced that such economic co-operation between our two countries will be advantageous as regards Japan's own economic prosperity.

Looking to the future, China has set itself the target of quadrupling its gross industrial and agricultural production by the year 2000. In this paper I should like to examine the feasibility of attaining this target by explaining the present state of China's energy and technology structures, and the major problems associated with these. A clearer understanding of China's economy seen from this dual viewpoint of energy and technology will, I feel, aid both of our countries in finding a way to effectively promote economic and technological exchanges, thus strengthening future relations between us.

Energy structure

According to recent studies, it will only be possible to double, not quadruple, China's energy output by the end of this century. Therefore, our problem is how to achieve a quadrupling of industrial and agricultural production with only a doubling of energy production. To do this, we must study structural energy policies that will enable the realization of our production target. As far as we know, a quadrupling of production within twenty years with only a doubling of energy is unprecedented in history. Can this unprecedented feat be accomplished under China's present conditions?

When considering this energy policy issue, we must keep in mind that the energy outlook for China is good. First, the coal situation: China's total coal reserves are estimated at 5 billion tons, which is the second largest reserve in the world. The retrievable coal reserves are estimated to be 1.4 billion tons, which is the third largest in the world. And the amount which has already been confirmed is 40,000 million tons, about enough to satisfy demand over the next twenty years.

Next, we have water-power resources. The water-power resources that China can develop come to nearly 400 million kilowatts. Only 5 per cent of this has been developed, but since the development rate in the industrialized countries is over 40 per cent, it can be said that China's potential development growth rate is very high.

Thirdly, oil: China currently has over 60,000 million tons of oil deposits, excluding offshore oil-fields. In addition, the conditions for nuclear power generation are also good: there are considerable deposits of uranium and production levels are high.

We must not, however, overlook the fact that these energy resources are unevenly distributed. Though China is rich in coal, it is mainly found in Shanxi province and Inner Mongolia, that is to say, the north-western part of the country. Recently, good coal veins have also been found in Guizhou. This will have great importance when we build thermal power plants there in the future. But even then we will not be able to remedy effectively the uneven distribution of energy resources. The major water-power resources lie in the south-west area; the major tributaries of the Chang Jiang (Yangtze Kiang), the Sanxia ('three canyons' of the Yangtze), and the Hongshui (a river in Guangxi where a thermal power station is now being constructed) are all located in that area. This unevenness is disadvantageous for the development and utilization of energy. For instance, the transportation of coal poses a major problem, and although we may build a large hydro-electric power plant in the south-west, transmission of electricity is a further complication.

To ensure the realization of these economic targets, we must chose an energy policy appropriate for China and its present situation, and create a rational structure for energy production and consumption. China should use coal as the main long-term energy source; in other words, both energy production and consumption should be based on coal. There is, however, controversy over whether this is the best choice. For instance, some say that we should rely on hydro-electricity. Although only 5 per cent of China's water supply has been developed, we see great potential growth, so an energy structure based on hydro-electricity might seem quite feasible. In reality, however, this is not a possible solution, because at present hydro-electricity accounts for only about 4 per cent of China's energy production and consumption. So even if we do emphasize the construction of hydro-electric power plants and manage to raise the proportion of hydro-electricity in the nation's power supply, it still cannot become the major long-term energy resource. There is no doubt that coal must form the foundation of China's energy production and consumption structures. In saying this, though, I do not mean to suggest that we underestimate the importance of developing alternative energy resources, such as water power.

Next, oil: unfortunately, we must admit that this is not a possible contender from the long-term viewpoint. China can only maintain the production of 100 million tons of inland oil per year, and giant new oil-fields – like Daqing – are no longer being discovered. Given these circumstances, maintaining an output of 100 million tons requires an additional oil production capacity of 8 to 10 million tons.

Since constant drilling for oil decreases underground oil pressure, less oil is obtained and the output from old fields decreases. To maintain a high underground pressure, water is injected, but this process itself requires electricity. Since more energy is needed to produce the oil, oil costs soar. From this it can be seen that China's provisional figures for oil production in the 6th five-year plan are not conservative at all. There is thus a need to discover new oil-fields and, at the same time, secure oil-fields ready for immediate use. In recent years, inland oil reservoirs have been found in places such as the southern part of Xinjiang, but we are not yet able to exploit those reservoirs to immediately increase our oil output. The drilling for offshore oil deposits has begun, and we have high hopes for its future, but since such exploitation is limited by high costs, as well as insufficient technological expertise and funds, we have no other choice but to co-develop these reserves with other countries. We have started test-drilling in some areas, but we still have a long way to go before large-scale production and utilization of these resources can be established. We cannot hope for such offshore oil during the course of the 6th five-year plan, but perhaps in the latter half of the 7th five-year plan, or in the 1990s, we may see the possibility of oil production of the order of tens of millions of tons. In conclusion, though, oil will not be a major energy source for a long time.

It has been suggested that China could follow the Japanese

model of development. Although Japan does not possess many natural resources, her industries – especially the petrochemical industry – have developed as a result of large oil imports. From this we can conclude that a country's energy structure need not necessarily be based on domestic natural resources. As you know, China is a populous, socialist state; from our experiences with revolution and construction, we have proved that unless we maintain the principle of 'self-reliance', production cannot develop smoothly. Therefore, when discussing energy policies designed to enable us to realize our economic targets, we must start thinking along the lines of self-reliance. Since we do not have surplus foreign currency, we cannot import much oil; this makes it impossible for us, in a short span of time, to introduce and build a larger number of advanced petrochemical facilities that can utilize imported oil more effectively. So, given China's present circumstances and future prospects, an energy structure based on oil is improbable.

We must accurately assess the drop in global oil prices over the last two years. This is another complicated issue, but I will outline the basic situation. The dramatic drop in global oil prices can be traced to the increase in oil production by non-OPEC countries – Britain, the Soviet Union and Mexico – energy-saving technology that appeared as a result of the high oil prices of the early 1970s, the development of alternative energy sources, and the crumbling of the OPEC monopoly because of domestic economic problems and discrepancies between member countries. But oil is a limited resource, a versatile and high-quality source of energy. So, in the long term, oil prices have a good chance of gradually rising again, with neither the sudden surge experienced during the 'oil inflation' period, nor the ensuing plunge. If this view is correct, there is no guarantee that China can use this global oil to her benefit, although it is said to be growing cheaper by the day.

The points that I have covered illustrate the necessity for China to implement and maintain an energy production and consumption structure based on coal.

Next, let us consider another important energy policy issue. By the end of this century, China's energy output will grow from an equivalent of 600 million tons of standard quality coal to more than 1,200 million tons. We confront the problem of how to guarantee the growth of the gross industrial and agricultural production from 715,900 million yuan in 1980 to 2.878 billion yuan in the year 2000 with only this limited increase in energy output. In order to accomplish this, besides selecting an energy structure based on coal, we must adopt a two-track strategy that allows for the simultaneous implementation of two policies at once. On the one hand, we must strive to develop new energy resources, though this is always limited by natural resource conditions and hampered by capital investment, economic and technological factors. During the 6th five-year plan, the government has been constructing several hydro-electric plants, large-scale coal mines, and nuclear power stations, all of which represent important progress towards the development of primary energy. On the other hand, we must conserve energy and increase the efficiency with which it is used. To achieve this, we must not only improve administrative control to abolish waste, but also continue making technological innovations, actively developing and promoting new technologies for energy conservation in order to further increase efficiency. We anticipate that we will be able to secure about half of the energy required to sustain the planned quadrupling of production as a result of this output increase, and the other half by conserving energy with new technologies and by increasing the amount of products with higher added value.

We must be aware of the problem of energy wasted through mismanagement, but I should also like to point out that we must fully recognize the fact that old technologies and facilities may also cause wastage. When compared to the industrialized countries, this latter type of energy wastage is prominent in China; therefore, there is considerable potential for boosting efficiency through renovation. Improving management practices, of course, is also important in energy conservation. After improvements of this nature have been made, the focus of conservation efforts will inevitably move to the new technologies. The one million *Jiefang* ('Liberation') vehicles being driven in China today consume 20 per cent more petrol than comparable models in the industrialized countries. The extra amount of petrol thus consumed is estimated to be of the order of one million tons. However, in the last two years we have refitted 220,000 of these *Jiefang* cars, reducing petrol consumption by

10 per cent. The amount thus saved in one year comes to 130,000 tons; so, if we manage to reduce consumption by 20 per cent and reach the level of efficiency enjoyed in the industrialized countries, we will be able to save more than 200,000 tons of petrol per year. Recently, engineers at Automobile Factory No. 1 in Changchun have developed a new lorry which uses 26 per cent less fuel than previous models. Furthermore, the government has already ordered a ban on the use of the old-type boilers that have a heating efficiency of only 30–40 per cent. There are 60,000 of these in China and, compared to the newer models that have a heating efficiency of 70–80 per cent, the old models consume an extra 4 million tons of coal per year. China currently has 200,000 boilers with an average heating efficiency of 55 per cent; if we refit them all to raise efficiency by 20–30 per cent, we will save 40 million tons of coal annually.

The development and promotion of energy-saving technologies is the only way to conserve energy and increase efficiency. Naturally, as energy-saving technologies become more sophisticated, the hopes for better management will rise. We choose to emphasize the technological solutions, but this does not mean that we are ignoring management techniques. No matter how high the quality and efficiency of the vehicles used to transport products may be, if there is poor management in the product supply mechanism, energy will be wasted in distribution, and efficiency levels will remain low. There is an obvious necessity for the scientific management and maintenance of new facilities for energy conservation.

If we are to adopt this two-track strategy that I have just explained, achieving quadrupled production with doubled energy is possible. However, this is not easy to accomplish, since we start at a very low point and our energy efficiency is lower than that in the industrialized countries. China is third in the world in energy consumption, but 113th in terms of GNP per unit of energy consumption. Furthermore, our energy consumption per dollar of GNP is 2.6 times that of India. According to statistics, energy consumption per hundred million dollars of GNP in terms of standard quality coal is 210,000 tons in China, 120,000 tons in the USSR, 91,000 tons in the US, and 37,000 tons in Japan. China consumes 600 million tons of coal per year, a figure roughly equivalent to Japan's consumption, though the GNP resulting from this energy is only one quarter of that of Japan, and gross national income is only one third of Japan's. Despite the presence of incomparable factors such as cost, quality, and differences in economic structure, this does serve to illustrate how poorly energy is utilized in China. But, as I have explained, we can be sure that there is considerable potential for raising efficiency. This plan to achieve quadrupled production by saving energy and raising efficiency is not the result of wishful thinking; it is a policy which reflects the real potential that lies within our nation.

Table 1   Relationship between the growth of industrial production and that of energy consumption.

		Industry		Primary Energy		ECE
		Index	Growth rate %	Index	Growth rate %	
USSR	1950–70	6.4	9.7	3.7	6.8	0.70
	1960–79	3.9	7.4	2.4	4.75	0.64
Japan	1960–79	6.0	9.95	4.0	7.5	0.75
China	1980–2000	4.5*	7.9*	2.1*	3.8*	0.48*

*projections

Note: Index figures represent the multiple by which industrial production or energy consumption increased; average growth rates are calculated on an annual basis for the specified period; ECE (elastic coefficient of energy) is calculated by dividing energy consumption growth rate by industrial production growth rate.

Nevertheless, we do not underestimate the magnitude of the difficulties which face us in this undertaking. The quadrupling of industrial production with only a doubling of energy output – and within a period of only twenty years – is unprecedented. As can be seen from Table 1, the Soviet Union increased its industrial production by a factor greater than six in the period 1950–70, but this was achieved with a quadrupling of energy output; from 1960 to 1979, industrial output nearly quadrupled, but with more than a doubling of energy. Japan's industry grew by six times and its primary energy by four times in the years 1960–79. For China to realize its target of quadrupled production, we must achieve an elastic coefficient of energy (ECE) of 0.48, a figure that is much lower than that seen in the Soviet Union and Japan in the 1970s. This is despite the fact that Japan is a country which possesses considerable know-how and technology in the field of energy conservation. Obviously the realization of our goal is not a simple matter.

In recent years, many people have commented that China's ECE must already be sufficiently low to achieve its aims. Indeed, a few years ago it sank to below 0.33, which was lower than all predictions for the end of this century. However, this was a temporary aberration, the result of measures taken to adjust China's economic and manufacturing structures as a means of tiding the country over during a period of energy supply difficulties. These measures included the drastic cutting of production of goods which required high energy consumption, and a simultaneous increase in the manufacture of light industrial products. According to long-term data compiled both within and without the country, the ECE has fluctuated around the level of 1.0 for a long time. In the past twenty years, due to technological innovations the trend was towards a figure slightly under 1.0. Given the present circumstances, our target of 0.48 is a plausible figure, but one that will demand great effort to attain.

Up until now, the 'energy' to which I have been referring is primary energy. Hydro-electric and nuclear power generation are sources of such primary energy, while traditional thermal power generation is an example of a secondary energy source. Now, in order to quadruple production, it is not enough merely to double primary energy output – from 300,000 million kWh to 600,000 million kWh – by the end of this century. According to the experiences of various countries, including China, in industrial development the elastic coefficient of electricity (electricity consumption growth rate / industrial production growth rate) is usually 1.0 or larger over a long period, and it seldom falls below this figure. Therefore, we cannot set our target below this figure without taking significant steps to put it there. For this reason, we must do our utmost to boost electricity output by four times or more. If we succeed in raising output from the present 300,000 million kWh to 1.2 billion kWh by the year 2000, we will have enough electricity to satisfy the needs of the developing economy. Thus, although the amount of energy required per unit of gross industrial production will decrease, the proportion of electrical power will increase; this is the natural result of mechanization and automation. China is lagging behind in electrical power generation; at the same time, demand for industrial and agricultural electrical power has surged, as has household consumption in both urban and rural areas due to the growing popularity of electrical appliances. Under these circumstances, even if we quadruple electrical power output by the end of the century, supply will still not catch up with demand. Although our energy structure will be based on coal for the remainder of this century, we can expect to see a rise in the proportion of electrical power in the energy structure.

To increase electrical power output, we must systematically plan the construction of several strategic, large-scale hydroelectric power plants, as well as those of a smaller scale. This is an essential and highly effective means of solving the electrical supply problems experienced by many farming regions. However, great care will have to be exercised in devising such plans, and attention should be especially paid to the development and utilization of water resources, including the role of water transport. We will probably also construct a number of thermal and nuclear power plants. China has already mastered the basic technologies involved in nuclear power generation, but since we have never implemented this knowledge, we lack the necessary experience. Also, difficulties are experienced in manufacturing some types of equipment. In order to construct nuclear power stations, it is necessary for us to introduce sophisticated technology from other countries, including that related to the disposal of nuclear waste. We have to give careful consideration to this problem. However, we can say that by planning the progressive development of technologies related to the harnessing of water power, thermal power, nuclear power, and other energy sources, it will be possible to quadruple electrical power output by the year 2000.

One issue that must not be overlooked in creating this energy structure based on coal is that of environmental pollution. With this in mind, we are trying to proceed in the direction of the hydrogenation and gasification of coal. These methods not only help to solve the environmental problem but also are very effective in facilitating the transportation of fuel. Technology for such processing is currently being actively studied in a number of countries, and China is co-operating with Japan in the development and trial operation of a small device capable of processing two hundred kilograms of coal a day. Coal is China's major energy source, and we must recognize the fact that unless this processing technology is developed, the environment may suffer considerable damage. Many innovations in the production and utilization of coal will be necessary.

Technology structure

At the 9th National Science and Technology Workers Forum, held in Beijing in 1982, Prime Minister Zhao Ziyang said that our economic targets may not be achieved without technological development; in other words, success requires progress.

Why do we value technological innovations so highly? To understand this, we should consider some possible development scenarios:

1   Even without any change in the level of technology, we can boost production solely through increases in labour and capital.

2   Even without any changes in technology, labour and capital, we can increase production by rationalizing production factors.

In both of these scenarios, however, the increase in production is limited. There is, though, a third possibility:

3   With changes in scientific knowledge and technology, there is no limitation to increases in production, because progress in science and technology is limitless.

It is for this reason that we have pinned our hopes on advances in science and technology as a means of attaining our economic targets. By the end of this century, we must absorb and disseminate throughout our country the technologies that the advanced countries obtained during the 1970s and 1980s.

Next, let us look at the role which technological innovations play in raising the productivity of labour. According to foreign statistics, technological advances are rapidly becoming a prominent factor in the increase of industrial productivity: at the turn of the century it accounted for 5–20 per cent, in midcentury this figure rose to 40 per cent, and in the 1970s it topped 60 per cent. At this moment, some advanced countries have already reached the position where 70–80 per cent of the rise in productivity is due to technological innovations.

Table 2   Countries which quadrupled their economies in a period of twenty years or less

	(years)	Growth rate %	Indicator
USSR	16	9.1	Gross Social Product
Bulgaria	15	10.6	Gross Social Product
Romania	15	9.9	Gross Social Product
East Germany	19	7.8	Gross Social Product
Japan	14	10.6	Gross National Product
West Germany	19	7.8	Gross National Product
Greece	20	7.4	Gross National Product

Note: Average growth rates are calculated on an annual basis.

Progress in science and technology has been shown to have accelerated the economic growth of some countries. As regards the period before the Second World War, the low level of technology can be cited as the reason why countries took so long to quadruple the size of their economies. It took Great Britain and France more than sixty years, Germany fifty-two years, and the United States thirty years to achieve this. After the war, however, there was a considerable speeding up, as can be seen in Table 2. The Soviet Union and several Eastern European countries, as well as Japan and West Germany, managed to quadruple their economies in less than twenty years. Even Greece accomplished this in twenty years. And one of the main reasons for this lies in the improvement of technology and the swift application of new technology to production. In the 1980s, science and technology are entering a new stage of development. Thus, it is with good reason that we are endeavouring to quadruple our production through the introduction of new technology.

Being a less developed country in a technological sense does have its advantages: we can save on the long years and high costs invested by the advanced countries which originally developed these sophisticated technologies. We have the privilege of choosing and introducing those that are most suitable for our needs. But of course there are also disadvantages. Since the level of education of the Chinese people is, on the whole, not very high, there is the problem of learning, mastering, and managing these advanced technologies. To overcome such basic problems, we must take appropriate measures to raise the overall level of understanding of cultural and scientific matters. Naturally we need to lay our foundations by implementing proper education, but when we consider the importance of science and technology in achieving targeted growth, we must realize that there are certain priority policies that need to be put into operation.

First, from now on the focus of our efforts to expand production will shift from the establishing of new industries to the upgrading of technologies used in existing industries; this approach will make use of the potential that already exists within the production system. Until recently, we have strived to increase production by constructing new industries; however, this required large infusions of capital, results were slow to materialize, and the whole approach was inefficient. While doing this we failed to pay proper attention to the renovation of the technology used in existing industries. Needless to say, I am not advocating a ban on the establishing of new industries, for there are still many gaps to fill. New technologies are appearing in rapid succession, and since it is necessary to strengthen our weak production sectors, we should continue to introduce new industries. That is to say, a balance must be struck: we will emphasize the upgrading of technologies used in existing industries, but continue to devote some of our energies to the introduction of new industries and technologies. By co-ordinating these strategies, we will be able to raise the hardware technology of the nation to new heights.

Next, the technology structure of society must be

rationalized and controlled. This structure may be defined in terms of many parameters, such as size of the work-force at each technological level, the product ratio of a specific technology to total production, the composition of technologies expressed in a specific manufactured item, and the ratio of technological assets (equipment) to total fixed capital assets. We have to address the problem of how to accurately adjust the changes in each technology to achieve our strategic target. This problem is in fact closely related to the issue of labour employment and, therefore, it is fitting that we should focus on the number of workers in each technological level, as expressed in Diagram 1.

Diagram 1   China's changing technology structure

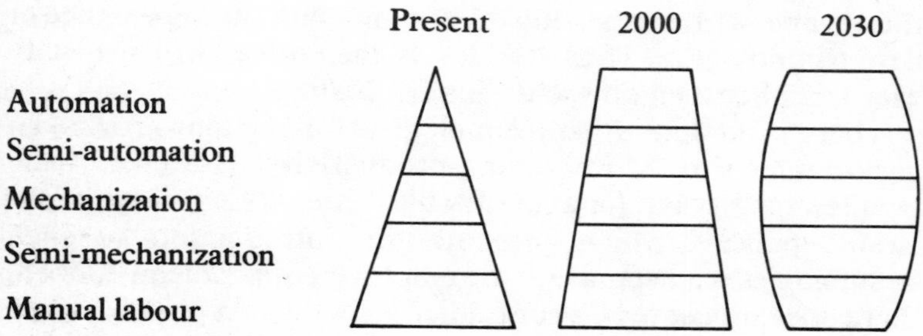

This model ignores the other possible parameters, the inclusion of which would naturally affect the shapes generated. In keeping with the classification system now used throughout the world, the technology structure has been divided into five different levels. At present, the shape of this structure is triangular but with the realization of our economic targets in the year 2000, it will have changed into a trapezium, or truncated triangle. Since China is a populous country with an overall low level of technology, there will no doubt still be a considerable amount of manual labour at the end of the century; this is why the base of the figure is still so wide. Despite this, the central and upper levels – representing automation, semi-automation, and mechanization – will have become relatively broad, representing a considerable improvement in the overall level of technology. This trapezium illustrates how China's unique technology structure will develop with the widespread introduction of the production technology employed by the advanced countries in the late seventies and early eighties.

Thirty years on, in 2030, the technology structure will have developed so as to resemble the barrel shape in Diagram 1. The two extremities are narrower than the centre, indicating a decrease in manual labour, but without so much broadening of automation that the structure becomes top-heavy. The reason for this is that the service sector, which is usually comprised of manual labour, is expected to expand greatly with the development of the economy. Something else which can be deduced from the model for 2030 is that China will catch up with the advanced countries in the field of applied science technologies.

It should, however, be borne in mind that the five different technological levels of Diagram 1 are not fixed and unchanging: they evolve with the passing of time and with the appearance of new technologies. Thus, the levels themselves will naturally vary from between now and the year 2030.

There is no doubt that technological innovations provide an important means of improving productivity. However, some people suggest that, for a country like China with its large population, policies which promote the introduction of such technologies may aggravate the employment problem. Indeed, there does appear to be a contradiction in this. At present, some enterprises which do not actually require a large work-force attempt to alleviate the employment problems of the young by over-hiring. This is a typical manifestation of the contradiction seemingly implied by trying to raise the levels of employment and productivity at the same time. Yet the fact is that these two policies need not contradict each other. The reason for this is simple. It is only when we succeed in increasing productivity in the manufacturing sector on a large scale that we can satisfy increasing demands for specific items. Once this has happened, its effects will be felt in the non-manufacturing sectors, in turn helping to develop education, culture, public health, science and technology, and physical education. The result will be an increase in the demand for labour in these growing sectors, and thus a rise in productivity in the manufacturing sector will have indirectly led to an increase in employment. A paradox does exist at present, and we cannot be sure when this will disappear, but we must not lose sight of the fact that our only hope for an increase in employment lies in an increase in productivity.

This link between productivity and employment is true not only of countries like China where the level of production is low, but also of countries like the United States. For instance, in the statistics supplied by Richard W. Riche in a 1983 article ('The Impact of Technological Change', *Economic Impact*, No. 41, 13–18) in the thirty-year period from the early fifties to the early eighties rapid American technological advances were accompanied by significant increases in productivity. Nevertheless, in no sector of the American economy except agriculture was there a decrease in the size of the work-force; in fact, there was even an increase. And in eight sectors – including mining, transportation, service, and government – over the thirty-year period one finds a doubling of the number of people employed. These statistics illustrate that advances in science and technology do not decrease the opportunities for employment; they only change the employment structure. Provided that the economy develops, there is no fire-and-water contradiction between policies that promote the introduction of advanced technologies to raise productivity and those that foster increased employment. What is true is that the relative work-force size of each sector will change, with the number of employees in the manufacturing sector probably decreasing.

We can thus conclude that a policy which forces workers into factories and ignores the potential for increased productivity via advanced technology is, from the long-term perspective, in effect closing the door to further employment, instead of opening it. Of course, I am not condemning attempts to find jobs for people; this is one of the responsibilities of a socialist state and it is necessary for the preservation of civil peace. When we set our economic targets, we knew that the road to greater employment lay in the direction of increased productivity. We should realize that China, a country of 1,200 million people, can in this way solve the employment problem by the end of this century.

Turning to the division of the labour force among the primary, secondary and tertiary industries, we can deduce that as a modern economy develops, the relative size of the manufacturing sector gradually decreases. This is illustrated in the statistics for the United States and Japan presented in Table 3. Conversely, it is a principle of economic development that the number of people employed in the tertiary industry increases, and China cannot be an exception to this, despite the evidence in Table 4. The main reason why the size of our tertiary industry work-force has not changed is that productivity in the manufacturing sector has not increased very much. Also, the service sector – with 4.5 to 5 million workers – forms a large part of the tertiary industry, but it is included in the secondary industry when compiling statistics. This is because all enterprises in China, whether large or small, operate comprehensively, so little of the service industry exists in the form of independent enterprises in society.

Table 3   Changes in the industrial and employment structures of Japan and the United States

	Primary Industry		Secondary Industry		Tertiary Industry	
	A %	B %	A %	B %	A %	B %
USA						
1967	3.06	5.2	39.9	31.3	57.2	63.5
1978	2.80	1.8	30.4	29.9	66.8	68.3
Japan						
1965	8.1	24.6	54.5	19.3	37.4	13.9
1975	4.2	13.9	56.9	34.0	38.9	51.9

Note: Figures in A columns represent the percentage of GNP, while figures in B columns represent the percentage of the total work-force accounted for by each industry.

Returning to the subject of solving paradoxes, we must deal with the present reality of the situation by taking appropriate measures to find jobs for the young unemployed. We can, for example, rationalize the production, business and service aspects of both the collectively and individually run enterprises that are found in the cities. But there are also other measures, such as the creation of organizations for road maintenance or afforestation. There are many regions which require labour for the protection and development of beautiful mountains and riv-

Table 4   China's employment structure

	Percentage of the total work-force		
	Primary Industry	Secondary Industry	Tertiary Industry
1965	81.6	8.3	10.1
1979	72.5	15.8	11.7
1981	72.0	16.3	11.7

Note: This division of the total work-force into primary, secondary and tertiary industries is for the purpose of comparison with other countries.

ers. Naturally, in order to preserve the correct skill composition and age range of their labour force, enterprises must make a balanced decision regarding the required educational level of new employees and the number to be hired. New enterprises will undoubtedly need a large number of new workers. It is clear that as science and technology continue to progress, the requirements for a grounding in scientific and cultural matters will rise accordingly. To comply with this trend, we will have to upgrade education and training programmes, as well as change part of the employment system.

Economic relations with Japan

There are nineteen countries or regional entities in the world which have managed to quadruple their economies within twenty years. Eleven of these are developing countries, with an average annual economic growth rate of 7.2 per cent, a level which is not too high for China to achieve. Although we foresee many difficulties in attaining our strategic target, we can count on China's superior socialist system, ample labour and natural resources; we can therefore say that there is a very high potential for economic growth.

Since December 1978, when the strategic policy for modernization was decided at the Third Plenary Session of the 11th National Congress of the Chinese Communist Party, our country has been steadily progressing on the path towards a healthy economic development. The international environment is also relatively encouraging. Therefore, as long as we continue to develop towards increased economic efficiency, adhering to the policy of opening the country to the outside and promoting further co-operative relationships with Japan and other countries in the technological and economic fields, we can be sure of attaining China's strategic target for economic development by the end of this century.

From the re-establishment of diplomatic relations, economic relations between China and Japan have made great progress. After the drop in trade over the previous few years, the total trade between these two countries in 1983 once again topped the 10,000 million dollar mark, registering a 12.8 per cent increase over 1982. With economic co-operation reaching new heights, this Sino-Japanese trade relationship significantly improved in both volume and quality. Japan's total exports for 1983 were 5.8 per cent up on 1982, but in fact its exports to China had risen by 40 per cent. The first long-term yen loans of the Overseas Economic Co-operation Fund and the energy resources development loans of the Export–Import Bank of Japan which were extended by Japan to China have been used mainly for the development of oil and coal resources, electrical power generation facilities, and transportation systems related to these. Furthermore, these construction projects have helped to promote further bilateral trade, both directly and indirectly. This illustrates the fact that the requirements of China's modernization and construction programme have served as a momentous spur to technological and economic co-operation between China and Japan. The future is decidedly bright. Our country is lacking in technology and capital, as well as expertise in modern administrative methods, and thus must actively seek out and absorb these through ties with other countries.

Of course, there are many differences between our countries' political systems, levels of economic development, national traits and customs, and these should be taken into consideration. They may indeed create some problems for bilateral economic exchanges. However, we enjoy a long history of friendly ties, of cultural and economic exchanges. The peoples of both our countries love peace and yearn for friendship. With a considerable foundation thus in place, we can say that all these factors create most advantageous conditions for future economic co-operation. So for this reason, no matter how many differences exist between the industrial and technological structures of China and Japan, there is great potential for co-operation in many fields. We are now witnessing a new technological revolution on a worldwide scale, one that is spurring on a readjustment of Japan's industrial structure, and this too can be turned to advantage via the greater rationalization of our economic ties.

By further developing our combined trade and technology exchanges, and searching for new ways to promote joint projects, China and Japan hope to establish an economic co-operation system that will be stable and long-lasting. This is directly linked to the stability of our own relationship, and can even be said to contribute to the peace and stability of Asia and of the rest of the world. The economic development of China and Japan will play an extremely important role in the development of the whole Asian region.

Oceania and the new artists

ALBERT WENDT

Introduction

> *These islands rising from wave's edge blue with*
> *brooding in orchid, fern and banyan, fearful gods*
> *awaiting birth from blood clot, into stone image*
> *and chant . . .*
> Albert Wendt, 'Inside Us the Dead'

I belong to Oceania, that vast stretch of the Pacific Ocean which encompasses Polynesia, Melanesia, and Micronesia – atolls and volcanic islands populated by just over five million people possessing a cultural diversity more varied than most other regions in the world.

I belong to Oceania, with its rich variety of philosophies and different ways of seeing and interpreting the human condition in relation to nature and the gods and the cosmos.

I belong to Oceania with its multiplicity of social, economic and political systems all undergoing different stages of decolonization, ranging from politically independent nations – including Western Samoa, Fiji, Papua New Guinea, Tonga, Vanuatu, the Solomons, Kiribati, Tuvalu and Nauru – through self-governing ones – Niue, and the Cooks – and colonies (mainly French and American).

I belong to Oceania, with its over 1,200 indigenous languages – plus English, French, Hindi, Spanish, and various forms of pidgin – and its rich variety of artistic expression.

I belong to Oceania – or at least I am rooted in a fertile portion of it – and it nourishes my spirit, helps to define me, and feeds my imagination.

I will not pretend I know her in all her manifestations. No

one – not even the gods – ever did; no one does; no one ever will, because whenever we think we have captured her she has already assumed new guises. The love affair is endless, because she is always changing. In the final instance, all countries, cultures, nations, and planets are only what we imagine them to be, at any chosen time. One human being's reality is another's fiction. Perhaps we ourselves exist only in one another's dreams.

All of us, in our various groping ways, are in search of that heaven, that Hawaiki, where our hearts will find meaning; most of us never find it, or at the moment of finding it, fail to recognize it. At this stage in my life, I have found it in Oceania.

Traditional arts and artists

Even though the types of arts and artists differ from culture to culture and from country to country, for the arts to flourish they need economic, social, intellectual and – above all else – spiritual sustenance.

Like a sensitive plant, the artist, through an unconscious process of osmosis, draws his mana (his artistic and imaginative energy) from everything surrounding him – the aesthetic and cultural traditions into which he is born, his personal relationships, even the food and drink he consumes. This mana he transmits back into his community in a reconstituted form. How well he does this depends on his talents and the ability of his society to receive his painting, or poem, or song, or whatever form he has encapsulated his mana in. Factors such as censorship, the reaction of critics or those who control his community and the art market, and the need to earn a living can influence, hamper, and even stop that transmission.

Before the coming of the 'Papalagi' (Europeans), the position and role of artists in Oceania varied from society to society. However, it can be said that they shared our societies' basic values, beliefs, and ways of viewing reality.

It is almost impossible now for any of us who have been brought up on Christianity and the Papalagi view of reality to reach back into our pre-Papalagi societies and understand how our ancestors saw themselves and the universe. We can only speculate imaginatively.

Our pre-Papalagi ancestors knew little science but they knew much about human experience. When we look at their societies, we cannot separate so-called religion and art from their total way of living and seeing. Everything was of one process: the web that was the individual person was inseparable from the web of *aiga* (clan) and village or tribe, which were inseparable from the web of *atua* (gods) and the animate and inanimate and the elements and the total web that was the cosmos. All were one in an organic process endowed with sacredness or mana. All was one living being, the unity-that-is-all; there was no dualism of subject and object, no 'I' or ego separate from an outer world that the 'I' can measure in separate parts, subdue, exploit and conquer. Their view of reality was mythos, the opposite of Western rationalism. Mythos does not try to replace experience; it gives it depth, vitality and value. Our pre-Papalagi ancestors' prayers, chants, incantations and myths are examples of mythos.

Because the pre-Papalagi artists shared our societies' ways of viewing reality, it was not difficult for them to express our societies' aspirations, visions, fears, hopes and dreams. In turn, it was easy for our societies to understand their symbolism and imagery. They worked – almost exclusively – for our societies, producing what our societies needed. And the deeper that need was for the artists, the higher their status was. Their work was predominantly directed towards ritual, magic and everyday living. The arts were not for their own sake but to serve society. Over the centuries, art styles changed slowly.

Then the reefs broke open: the Papalagi sailed into our lives.

Colonialism: Western thought and rationalism

Throughout history, human beings have pondered these basic questions: What are we doing on this planet? What is our planet doing in this universe? What is our universe, what is it made of, and how does it work? If we, our planet, and our universe are going anywhere, where are we going?

Every group of people evolves its own languages to answer these questions. We see through those languages or structures.

Or, to put it another way, we impose them on what we see. Western rationalism emerged in Europe as the predominant way of seeing. When the Papalagi colonizers came to Oceania, they brought with them that view of reality.

This view has its roots in the Renaissance, the return to Greek learning and the decline of the Church's power in Europe. The Greek mode of thought became the basis of Western thought, which assumes that only 'being' is, and that there is a world separate from the self. The Church's power declined even more drastically when Copernicus discovered that the Earth was not the centre of the Universe. Even God's central position became insecure. And as the Papalagi discovered more planets and an infinity of universes, some of them pronounced God dead.

When René Descartes declared, 'I think therefore I am', he enthroned Reason as the way of giving meaning to man and his universe. Descartes saw the universe as a Great Machine which could be studied, and understood, in all its separate parts. The question in science was to discover how this machine worked.

Isaac Newton was the first to formulate the laws by which the machine operated. He gave mathematical expression to principles which unify large areas of experience. He gave the Papalagi a powerful tool and instrument for studying, measuring, and conquering their environment. The industrial and scientific revolutions of the eighteenth and nineteenth centuries in Europe were built on this.

Cartesian logic and Newtonian physics see reality in a deterministic way: as soon as the universe was created everything that was to happen was already predetermined – nothing can be changed. The machine operates according to its own laws, and human beings are cogs in it; freewill is an illusion. Darwin's theory of evolution and its accompanying philosophy of social Darwinism reinforced this rigidly deterministic view of reality.

The English missionaries and other Papalagi colonizers came to Oceania mainly during the latter half of the nineteenth century. It was the zenith of British world supremacy, when Britain was 'Great' and controlled the largest colonial empire ever carved out by any single power in human history. It was also the height of the Industrial Revolution and the euphoric belief that progress (English style) would save, from ignorance and pov-

erty, all peoples everywhere. Science, technology, British
know-how and ingenuity – founded solidly on the principle of
scientific objectivity – would overcome all barriers and solve all
problems. English missionary endeavour went hand in hand
with British trade and colonialism. Queen Victoria, progress,
thrift, hard work, cleanliness and godliness would conquer the
world for the Christian God; everything that was English and
godly was a blessing to be conferred on the benighted heathen.

Our early missionaries were humble folk, mainly tradesmen,
but they were Englishmen who viewed the world through their
Victorian Englishness, as it were – they could not do otherwise!
On the whole, they were courageous, hard-working, persistent.
Their view of reality was based on rationalism and whatever
brand of Christianity they believed in; they were convinced that
by converting us to their view they were saving us, the 'wilder-
ness', from Darkness.

Reality is what we take to be true. We see what we believe. As
was to be expected, anything in our Oceanic cultures which did
not fit into the colonizers' reality was outlawed, banished to the
realms of the supernatural and the mystical, dismissed as super-
stition and ignorance, or not seen at all. Most of our ancestors
accepted the conversion to that reality readily, gladly. Many of
them were sent as missionaries to convert the rest of the pagan
Pacific.

Papalagi rationalism and thought imprisoned our ancestors
in the symbolic, reduced their world from the pure awareness of
experience to the confines of symbols. 'In the beginning was the
Word, and the Word was with God, and the Word was God.'
Our Oceanic ancestors' way of seeing – derived from thousands
of years of human experience and knowing the unity-that-is-all
– was declared inadequate, deficient, because it was considered
'illogical' in the light of the Word.

By radically changing or destroying the religious and social
context in which our artists worked and from which they
derived their mana, colonialism – whether it was British,
American, French or Spanish – killed the inspiration and the
well-springs of many of our traditional arts. The colonizers,
especially the missionaries, also condemned and banned much
of our art as being 'pagan and licentious'. As a poet friend once
put it, 'The missionaries came with the Bible in one hand and

the chisel in the other!'

Colonialism shattered the reefs of our enclosed, slowly changing traditional world, bringing with it a bewildering farrago of new values, attitudes, ideas, images and symbols, new technologies, and ever-changing art styles, fads and fashions, which for a long time threw our traditional artists off balance, and, in many cases, destroyed them.

As the members of the community, their audience, became converted to Christianity and sought the new ways and cargo of the Papalagi, our traditional artists were valued less and less. In short, they lost their clientele and consequently their livelihood.

It was inevitable, therefore, that the vitality and artistic standards of most of our traditional arts would decline tragically.

Recovery: the new artists

In some of our countries, we are just starting to recover from that decline. This cultural renaissance – inspired, fostered and led mainly by our own people – will not stop at the artificial political frontiers drawn by the colonial powers. It is enriching our cultures further, reinforcing our identities, our self-respect and our pride, and taking us through a genuine decolonization. It is also acting as a unifying force in our region.

The rate of recovery and healing depends on many factors: on how fast political decolonization occurs, on how fast our peoples recover their pride and actually seek to establish new identities and shape their own destinies, on the dedicated work of art catalysts, on individual artists encouraging others, on enlightened political leaders and educational policies and curricula, and on the availability of patronage and a sympathetic art clientele.

Today you can travel throughout Oceania (including New Zealand and Australia) and find, proliferating everywhere, international arts and crafts geared to the tastes of outsiders, especially tourists. Dance, music, architecture, and even food are affected.

The promoters of this art claim that it is solid proof of an artistic revival.

Art objects in our pre-Papalagi societies had a meaning directly related to our societies. The clients who now want these traditional objects do not understand or care about their traditional functions; they want what they deem to be 'authentic traditional art'. And the more sensational and grotesque and exotic these objects are, the better. So, to stay alive, our artists and craftsmen produce lifeless imitations and much inferior art.

The trend is intensifying because tourists want this art: masks, lampshades, spears, tikis, war clubs, crocodiles and turtles and other creatures not of Oceania, carvings of every size and shape, and copies upon copies of African and Asian carvings. Our artists are even giving tourists the exaggeratedly 'primitive'.

This tourist art is acting as a major barrier to the emergence of a vital Oceanic art that reflects our present societies and realities in truly unique Oceanic ways, styles, images, and symbols – in languages that are derived from our individual identities.

Colonialism, by shattering the world of the traditional artist, also broke open the way for a new type of artist who is not bound by traditional styles and attitudes, who explores his individuality, experiments freely and expresses his own values and ideas, his own mana unfettered by accepted conventions: the artist who casts himself adrift in the void and plots his own course by discovering and developing his own vision, voice, style.

This happened, and is happening, with greater intensity in some parts of Oceania than in others. It is associated primarily with the towns, the rise of nationalism, and the search for identity. The most exciting developments in art are occurring in New Zealand – among the Maoris – and in Papua New Guinea.

Apart from the Australian aboriginals, the Maori people have suffered more from colonialism than any other Oceanic people. At the start of this century, it was feared that the Maori people were dying out. Up until the Second World War, Maori art was in a serious decline. However, the post-war period has witnessed a rapid recovery in population, large-scale movement into the cities, and an ever-increasing entry of Maoris into training colleges, universities and art schools. As a result of this and the accompanying exposure to international art, there has been a dynamic rebirth of Maori art. We are seeing a flowering of major talent using both traditional and new media, and exploring numerous themes, ideas, and styles which range from the traditional to the international. Most of the artists are influenced by international art styles. All are conscious of their Maori identity.

Papua New Guinea developed perhaps the richest and most diverse traditional art in the world. The new art began to emerge in the 1960s and was associated with the rapid rise of nationalism, the opening of the University of Papua New Guinea, the work of catalysts like Ulli and Georgina Beier, the establishment of the Creative Arts Centre (now the National Art School), and the rise of leaders – like Michael Somare – who see art as a positive way of forging a national identity for Papua New Guinea.

The new artists come mainly from cultures without strong traditional arts, or from those whose artistic traditions have been undermined. Papua New Guinea today has artists of international standing: Kauage, Akis and Jakupa, for example. A rich and distinctively Papua New Guinean imagery and symbolism, which transcends the numerous individual PNG cultures, has emerged. The new artist is New Guinean.

In other Oceanic countries the picture, as far as art is concerned, is not so encouraging. The difficult work of discovering and sustaining new artists, and of developing imaginative art programmes in schools has only just begun. Already, however, some modern artists of standing have emerged: Aloi Pilioko of Wallis, Iosua Toafa and Sven Orquist of Western Samoa, and Kuai Maueha of the Solomons. These artists are forging distinct styles to suit not only their individual visions, but also the artistic traditions of their countries.

Developments in the other arts

Exciting developments are also occurring in some of the other arts. Those traditional art forms which have, despite colonialism, remained relevant to our societies and our everyday lives have continued to thrive. Every four years we hold a South Pacific Festival of Arts to which Oceanic countries send dancers, musicians and artists. So far, these festivals have shown that Oceanic dance, song-making and music have remained the strongest art forms.

Some of our countries now have national dance theatres which are recognized internationally. Songs and dances are being renewed, revised, and experimented with constantly in order that they may reflect the moods, spirit, problems, and feelings of our present societies.

Up to about the 1960s, nearly all of the literature about Oceania was written by Papalagi and other outsiders. Our islands were – and still are – a gold-mine for foreign novelists and film-makers, bar-room journalists and semi-literate tourists, sociologists, anthropologists, ethnomusicologists, PhD students, sailing evangelists, UNO experts and colonial administrators, together with their well-groomed spouses. Much of this literature ranges from the hilariously romantic, through the pseudo-scholarly, to the infuriatingly racist: from Margaret Mead's free-loving Samoans; Somerset Maugham's puritan missionaries, drunks and saintly whores; and James Michener's rascals and golden Hawaiians; to the stereotyped childlike pagan who needs to be steered to the Light. The Oceania found in this literature is more revealing of Papalagi fantasies and hang-ups, of their prejudices and ways of viewing the crippled cosmos, than of our actual islands.

Since the 1960s, a literature written by our own writers has emerged.

In Papua New Guinea a modern literature grew quickly. Now there are novelists: Vincent Eri, Russell Soaba and John Kolia; poets: John Kasaipwalova and Apisai Enos; and a play-wright: Karma Kepi.

Two of New Zealand's major poets are Alistair Campbell, of Cook Islands descent, and Hone Tuwhare, a Maori. There are the Maori novelists and short-story writers Patricia Grace, Witi Ihimaera and Keri Hulme.

The same growth is being experienced in the other countries of Oceania. The most recent development is the growth of literature in our indigenous languages.

The writer as the new artist

When one talks about the game of writing, the term 'game' implies that the writing of fiction is enjoyable and played according to certain rules. There is much truth in that. At times, when the writing is going well and the images and characters are writing themselves out – through me – on to the page, I do find the game enjoyable, even euphoric. But the rewriting, over and over again, in an attempt to bring it closer to my expectations of perfection is, for this player, quite painful. Though I suppose that in every sport one has to have – apart from a little talent and luck – a lot of stamina and tenacity, plus the masochist's ability to absorb pain, enjoyably!

Every time someone calls me a writer, I feel embarrassed. It is an accolade I do not deserve. But I do write, and I have been trying to write – part-time – for over twenty years now. It is only a part of my life, yet it is becoming a very important part because I am now into my second adolescence, otherwise known as middle age, and have need of status props to support my ulcerated soul and self-esteem. I need an 'art' to justify my life, to persuade myself that I have not wasted the forty-three years I have been a wasteful passenger on this spaceship.

For me, writing has always been a game, an attempt to defeat gravity, to design a ball that when thrown up will not come down, to 'con' readers and listeners into believing in what I am conjuring up. Yet, even when I think I am fooling some people some of the time, I know – and enjoy knowing – that I am not fooling everyone all of the time!

A writer, like other artists, is a trickster, a *faitogafiti*. The more skilled and experienced he is at the game, the better he can hide his tricks. All my life I have admired confidence men, even mythical ones.

For me, the best writers are those who invent new tricks, and who – like the gifted *taulaaitu* or spirit mediums – weave new incantations to bring their worlds (shaped in their images) into being, and who can draw on rich veins of ore to do so. The weakest writers, although they may have a dazzling repertoire of tricks, use a lot of hot air to play the game with. Unfortunately, this is the fate of most writers, particularly those who live to write for a long time. We play lively, powerful tricks while we have a lot to say. Eventually, however, we all run out of fuel, yet we still go on using our polished tricks – to say nothing. This fear haunts all writers. And drives some of us to self-destruction.

In my arrogant misspent youth, I took the game too seriously: I considered it the preserve of a specially gifted 'nobility', a craft that would change the planet, perhaps heal it a little. At that stage, I was sure that writing would make me a person to be admired, and, of course, earn me an unlimited heaven of permanently suntanned goddesses. I did not realize that the game is one you have to play for a lifetime, compulsively, without the healing and the suntanned goddesses. And once hooked on it, it will not let go, even when it is killing you and your wife and whoever else is within range of your rampantly mushrooming disillusionment.

In the end it is like being a punch-drunk boxer: you react automatically to the bell and the blows, but you no longer have the fitness or brains to dodge, weave, and survive to describe the fight afterwards.

Writing, as the New Zealand poet Jim Baxter once told me, is like contracting the measles: we all get it once, but some of us never get over it.

I now know that my writing will not change very much. But then I also know that it is not that type of game. It is a game to entertain myself, to con myself into believing that it is all worthwhile, that I am more complete than I am. The game allows me to take the various roles of player, opponent, hero, victim, villain, executioner, umpire, winner and loser.

When I said that I have always admired confidence men, even mythical ones, I was thinking of the trickster Maui, who appears in different guises in all Polynesian mythologies. He is central to my game.

As you may know, Maui was the demigod who relished playing a kind of Russian roulette with the gods. He stole from them Fire, the War Club and the Planting Stick, and gave that marvellous technology to us so we could eat cooked flesh, club one another, and plant crops. When Ra, the Sun, went too fast across the sky for Maui's liking, he snared it, beat it, and made it promise to go slower.

Like all of us, though, Maui got carried away with his successes and decided to take on Hine-nui-te-Po, the death goddess. In this adventure, he took along his friends, the fantails, telling them to keep quiet while he made his merry way into the death goddess's womanhood. He was hoping to come out of her mouth – familiarity with basic anatomy not being one of his strong points!

While Maui was climbing the fantails laughed, awaking the goddess who, on finding him in there, crossed her legs, and thus ended Man's quest for immortality.

In Maui I see the writer, stealing – skilfully and daringly – all the gods' sacred possessions and giving them to mankind. If the writer has any guts, which is what all the great players in every sport need, he too will eventually dare Hine-nui-te-Po. And while he is in there, being ground to a delicious death, his friends – the fantails and readers – will be laughing their heads off.

It is all fiction anyway: birth, life, death, even the death goddess. We have to persuade ourselves that they are real and do exist. As Jorge Luis Borges has said, perhaps we exist only in one another's dreams. I am a player in your novel, your poem, your song. And you are a player in mine.

I have never really appreciated why some people – usually critics and academics, the supposedly skilled commentators on the sport – take the game so seriously, or at least give their readers and students that impression. Perhaps they have to; after all, they earn their living and reputations from it.

Even when I am in the suicidal throes of the bruising maul that is novel-writing, there is an insistently impish voice jabbing at my left ear drum: 'It is all pretence. Why are you being so serious?' 'Because I hate losing, *wantok*!' I reply. 'I hate losing to a novel that will not be born in the shape, size, smell, taste, sound and colour that I want it to!'

We go on playing because we have to, we hate losing. And perhaps because many of us are not much good at anything else! But I believe that we have got to play the game with commitment, nerve, gusto, growing skill, and a lot of cheating and imagination, improvising all the way. And, like most players, we may not be able to last the distance.

The writers who do last and survive, with some measure of dignity and grace, do so because they are able to bend or dictate some of the rules, and because they have the insane tenacity to keep challenging Hine-nui-te-Po.

Ultimately it is a lonely, financially unrewarding game. It is just you and the ravenously empty page.

By the way, when writers gripe about being underpaid, underfed, neglected, and badly in need of patronage, just remind them that no one forced them to become players; they chose that themselves.

Why a writer writes is not important, really. However, it is important that he writes, that he tries his best to catch his 'songs' and make them whole, and that in the process he develops other ways of transcribing, of purifying our language, of adding to it his own way of seeing and singing, of making us a little more articulate, more clear to ourselves.

If my main aim in writing was to make a lot of money, then the market would determine, to a large degree, what I write. We 'serious writers' keep telling ourselves and each other that using our talents to make money is uncivilized, barbaric. But secretly we envy Harold Robbins's Rolls-Royce, and his caviare-filled days in Cannes! We are also hurt – but try not to show it – when our comrades' books sell more copies than ours.

So if I do not write for the market, for whom do I write? When I was a romantic revolutionary, I used to tell myself that I was writing for myself. Eventually, though, I had to leave the womb and face the inevitable contradiction implied by wanting to have my work published. Why get your work published? Because, of course, you want to be read by someone else.

Every writer creates his own readership. At different stages of our lives we have our favourite authors and our favourite types of reading. I have never been keen on biographies, autobiographies, travel literature, dictionaries, most pre-twentieth-century fiction, Walt Whitman, Donald Barthelme, Enid Blyton, Richard Adams, and so on. Right now, I am 'into' – as my American friends would say – Italo Calvino, Gabriel Garcia Marquez, Walker Percy, Ōe Kenzaburō, Robert Stone, new Third World fiction, gory American crime fiction, and works explaining the latest findings in physics and biology. I try to read all new poetry, and everything written by Pacific islanders. I have gone off V.S. Naipaul, Solzhenitsyn, *Mad Magazine*, J.P. Donleavy, *Playboy* and the *Guinness*

Book of Records.

This sets me off on an interesting tangent. Ever since I saw my first movie when I was about nine years old, I have been addicted to films; that addiction continues to have a strong influence on my writing. Every time I travel abroad I try to see as many new films as I can. I also try to see as much art as I can, and that influences my work too.

But back to the question – who do I write for? I write for whoever reads my work, and for the Wendt faithfuls out there. The game seems worthwhile when readers write and tell me they enjoyed one of my books. Or when I am on a bus or an aeroplane and I see people with copies of my books. Or when I find out that my work is being studied in schools, training colleges and universities. Or when I notice the influence of my work in the work of other writers. It is good for the ego. It encourages me to go on playing the game, knowing that I am not just sending messages out into an uninhabited silence, that there are sympathetic receivers out there.

I cannot explain why I wrote what I have written over the years, except to say I think it has been an attempt to find out who I am: my beginnings, my diseases and gifts, the whys and wherefores of people. In that search, I have written mainly about my own people. I hope that I have helped to illuminate some aspects of their nature and, through them, the nature of people everywhere. I hope that I have also destroyed some of the stereotypes and fallacious myths about Samoa, Polynesia and the South Seas. And I pray that I have not replaced them with equally misleading ones.

Third World fiction is studied more in departments of sociology and anthropology than in literature departments. There is an enormous danger in this. Teachers and other readers go to my work for sociological and anthropological information, forgetting that it is fiction, that even most of the supposedly traditional myths in my work are figments of my imagination!

From a very early age I have suffered from a sense of unreality: a sense that I am not whole, or real, and that I live in a world which reflects this. It did not help that I left Samoa, my country, when I was thirteen and was 'adopted' by another language, English – New Zealand English, to be more accurate – and another culture. From these adopted parents I have inherited a love of sport (particularly Rugby), beer and New Zealand pub life, some typical New Zealand foods, and an irrepressible sense of fair play, of sticking up for the underdog and 'giving the other joker a fair go'. From these parents I have also acquired an unshakeable aversion to the middle-class fear of being adventurous when it comes to food, people, thought, politics, and most other things – including fiction.

I think that every time a writer tries to fish a poem or story out of the void, he is trying to complete himself. He is trying to create something that is whole, self-contained, unlike himself, an unbroken wholeness, a unity-that-is.

We know that language cannot be used to communicate experience, because words are symbols; they represent real things. The reality of symbols is an illusory reality. However, we cannot help living in that illusory reality – we have nothing else. So although the serious writer claims that his fiction penetrates illusion, can we say that he – more than anyone else – lives in an illusory reality because of the fact that he works with words and symbols? Or is he able to use symbols to penetrate our illusory reality and create a world closer to what really is?

Of all writers, I believe the poet is closest to what really is, for he tries to catch more wholly, less logically, more intuitively. He is made in Maui's image: son of a philandering god and a virgin earth-mother!

We Samoans can all trace our ancestry to certain gods although, alas, few of us are poets! Yet it perhaps explains why I obtain the greatest feeling of achievement when I manage to fish a poem out of my rib cage and recognize it as another step towards completing myself.

The university as an agent of change – the role of Japanese universities

RAYSON LISUNG HUANG

I am greatly honoured to be invited here to speak on the auspicious occasion of the 125th anniversary of the foundation of what was eventually to become your distinguished university. I am especially pleased to be here because of the link which has existed between this great institution and my own university, in Hong Kong, for many years past, in the form of exchange teachers who have benefited our academic curriculum and enriched our academic life. Especially in the fields of language studies and social sciences we have learned much from Japanese academics, among whom I should mention in particular Professor Nihei Yasumitsu of Keio University who has, for a number of years, paid us regular visits and contributed in a most valuable way to our teaching and research in economics.

When Fukuzawa Yukichi established what was to become Keio University at the start of the final decade of the Tokugawa shogunate, the dawn of 'enlightenment' – in the social and intellectual context in which we tend to use that word today – was only beginning to break on a world still in thrall to servitude and exploitation. In China, the Second Anglo-Chinese War was being temporarily concluded by the Treaty of Tientsin and the Taiping Rebellion, which was to be suppressed six years later with help from overseas, was well under way. In Russia, the death of Nicholas I three years earlier in 1855 had brought the more enlightened Alexander II to the throne, and with him hope for an end to long and brutal tyranny. But the emancipation of the serfs was still three years away. In Britain, the novels of Charles Dickens were gradually drawing attention to social evils; and in the United States Abraham Lincoln, who was already champion of civil liberties and was to be elected President in two years time, was being defeated in his bid for the

Senate. In the scientific arena, Charles Darwin and Dr A.R. Wallace were contributing a joint paper on the variation of species, a prelude to *On the Origin of Species*, published in the following year (1859). The civilized world was thus poised on the brink of exciting intellectual discovery, technological innovation and social reappraisal. But also straining at the leash were the dogs of war. It is one of the saddest reflections on the human condition that the pall of warfare, and ultimately the mushroom cloud of devastation, should be cast over a whole century to such an extent that positive achievements were to be completely overshadowed by bitterness and enmity among or even within nations. The American Civil War left a long aftermath of hatred and internecine feud. The horror of the European Holocaust burnt an unforgettable image on the conscience of the West. And, nearer home, for a period of fifty years from the end of the last century to the mid-1940s, the darkest page was written in the history of relations between two great nations of Asia, China and Japan. No one wins a war: there are merely degrees of loss; and the hurt, reproach and waste survive when little else does. To forget is impossible; indeed that is the way it should be, for only by remembering our mistakes and our past can we face the future realistically and hope to avoid repeating the wrongs. It is only within the last decade that, for our own region, the cloud has begun to lift and allowed us to see something of the panorama of world development and positive international progress.

I want to focus on part of that world scene – the part which concerns us most, our own region – on a vista now becoming apparent as the cloud of enmity begins to lift. I intend to highlight some of the positive contributions from certain quarters of Japan towards the promotion of goodwill with China during and prior to this period. As we shall see, these contributions played an important role in the formation of modern China.

For centuries before the Meiji Restoration the educational flow between China and Japan had mostly been one-way: students only went from Japan to China to study culture, literature and religion. There was an about-turn after the Meiji Restoration. Chinese intellectuals saw with approval the steady advance of Japan into the modern era. The readiness to experiment with new methods while adhering to traditional ideals and codes of behaviour appealed to such scholars as Zhang Zhidong (1837–1909) who saw the need to reform the social, educational and political system in China which was then under Manchu rule. Japan was becoming a world economic and political power without any apparent conflict in aims and outlook between the rulers and the ruled, and modernization did not jar the stability of society. The direction was firm, the pace unhurried and conservative. This relatively harmonious progress towards the twentieth century appealed to the Chinese reformers whose aim was to modernize China while retaining the monarchy. Liang Qichao (1873–1929) regarded Japan as a possible paradigm for China, and he and Kang Youwei (1858–1927) sought refuge in Japan after the so-called 'Hundred Days Reform' (Bairi Weixin) in the summer of 1898. The Dōbun Kai, founded in November 1898, was closely associated with a Chinese reform movement, a political party known under the name of Qiangxue Hui, which had gained the sympathy of many Japanese scholars and writers, especially among the Sinologues.

Although the efforts of reformers like Kang Youwei and Liang Qichao were thwarted by the Empress Dowager, the sympathy of the Dōbun Kai for the Chinese reform movement was not productive since it nurtured a seed which was not to come to fruition until later. In 1898, Ōkuma Shigenobu (1838–1922) put forward what later became known as the 'Ōkuma Doctrine'. This maintained that Japan, having managed to secure for herself the first benefits of modernization, should guarantee China freedom from Western aggression and should help in reorganizing her system of government and in overcoming her social inertia. Ōkuma believed that China would not remain quiescent forever, but that a hero would rouse her to her reformation. The advent of the hero would be accompanied by a surge of patriotism, and China would be restored to her place among the world powers. It was Ōkuma's view that Japan, by way of return for the benefits she had derived in the past from China's culture and spirit, should render assistance to the foreseen Chinese 'hero' in his efforts: China would then be both friendly and grateful to Japan. The search for this hero became the mission of people like Miyazaki Torazō (1872–1922). When Miyazaki met Sun Yatsen, better known as Sun

Wen, in Japan in Yokohama in 1897, he believed he had found the hero. It is interesting to note that the Chinese name Sun Zhongshan was derived from the Japanese name 'Nakayama' that Sun Yatsen adopted in his disguise as a Japanese to evade the detection of the Manchu government. Thus Japan can claim a part in Sun Yatsen's overthrow of the Manchus in 1911 and in the founding of the Republic of China. I should like to add a small Hong Kong footnote to this episode by mentioning that Sun Yatsen was from 1887 to 1892 a student at the Hong Kong College of Medicine and one of its first graduates. It was from this college that the University of Hong Kong was founded.

Many scholars from China were attracted to study in Japan during the Meiji period, most of them drawn by the more liberal educational system such as Fukuzawa established here at Keio. There is no need to remind anyone of Fukuzawa's aims and achievements; suffice it to say that the emphasis he placed on basic general education in the developing sciences and arts of modern civilization – ranging from mathematics and physics to social studies and languages – was new and exciting to the young intellectuals of China. In 1896 the Manchu government sent thirteen Chinese students, aged between 18 and 32, to study in Japan. Thereafter the number of Chinese students in Japan increased rapidly, to 200 two years later in 1898, and to 1,000 in 1903, swelling to about 8,000 in 1906 – a very large number by any standards.

Chinese students had, it is true, studied abroad before this period. The first Chinese student to go abroad was Rong Hong (Yung Hung; 1828–1912), who was sent to North America in 1846. It was at the instigation of Rong Hong that Zeng Guofan (1811–72) sent thirty Chinese students to study in the United States of America in 1872. A number of Chinese students had also been to Europe to study. In terms of numbers, however, Japan was soon far ahead of the other countries. The proximity of Japan helped of course, as did the much lower cost of living compared with the West. Furthermore, there was a much greater similarity of cultures and it was easier for Chinese to learn Japanese than English or any other European language.

But the great majority of Chinese students studying in Japan were private students, for Chinese government sponsorship still inclined towards the United States or even a European country, Germany for instance, rather than Japan. It thus came about that those students who went to North America or Europe were either government-sponsored or belonged to a higher or wealthier social class than those who studied in Japan. On their return to China the former found it easier to obtain employment and, having been government-sponsored students, they usually obtained better jobs. However, students returning from Japan excelled in their achievements. In a survey published in 1932, out of the forty-five leaders in the Chinese government, eighteen were educated in Japan, four were educated both in Japan and in Europe, six in the United States, one each in England, France and Germany, and fourteen had not received education abroad. Among writers, 155 out of a list of 322 published in 1937 had received education abroad. Among them, fifty-seven had returned from Japan, forty-eight from the United States, twenty from France, twelve from Soviet Russia, six each from England and Germany, two from Belgium, and the remaining four had been to more than one country, including Japan. Among the political leaders and military commanders in the Republic of China, Jiang Jieshi (Chiang Kai-shek; 1887–1975), He Yingqin (1889–), Yan Xishan (1883–1960), and Jiang Zuobin (1884–1942) all studied in a Japanese military school; Wang Jingwei (1883–1964), Hu Hanmin (1879–1935), Liao Zhongkai (1877–1925) and others studied at Hosei University. Japanese-educated Chinese also played an important role in the establishment of the People's Republic of China. Among them were Zhou Enlai (1898–1976), Dong Biwu (1885–1975), He Xiangning (1878–1972), and Liao Chengzhi (1908–83).

Generally speaking, in the long term China derived more benefit from her Japanese-educated students than from those who were educated in the West. For students in Japan continued to use the Chinese language much more than did their counterparts in Western countries who lived in the environment of an entirely foreign culture and who had to learn and use a language entirely different from their own. Because of the common use of Chinese characters, some Chinese students in Japan managed to communicate through a minimum amount of spoken Japanese, and at no stage did they ever think of foregoing the Chinese language. They thus retained strong ties and allegiance to their homeland and culture while benefiting from a broader-based education. Some students in Western countries, on the other hand, were overwhelmed by the material progress they saw, considering 'even the moon in the West rounder than the moon back home', to use a Chinese saying, and became somewhat alienated from their own cultural heritage. This caused some trepidation on the part of many parents intending to send their children to the West for education. In view of this, it is not surprising to find that the Japanese-educated Chinese students retained their attachment to their culture and language and that many became notable Chinese writers when they reached maturity.

When towards the end of the last century China finally began to replace her traditional educational system, it was largely from Japan rather than from the West that she drew most inspiration, though to a certain extent she was also influenced by Germany. In spite of its many failings, this new system of education instilled into the minds of the young Chinese a new sense of national awareness. Many textbooks at various levels were translated from Japanese into Chinese. Some of these had originally been written in a Western language – mostly English, German, and French. They had first been translated into Japanese, and then Chinese translations were made from the Japanese. Thus scholars today still remember the works of Wang Guowei (1877–1927) – the *Wang Guantang xiansheng quanji* (Taipei, 1968), the *Guantang jilin* (Beijing, 1961), and the *Luo Xuetang xiansheng quanji* (Taipei, 1968–76) – and Luo Zhenyu (1866–1940), for making accessible to them so many Chinese writings preserved in Japan but hitherto unknown to the Chinese. Though this is not to say that the Chinese did not translate directly from Western languages, translations from the Japanese certainly made up the majority of the output. Statistics given in the *Zhongguo jindai chuban shiliao* show that between 1901 and 1904, out of 533 translated works, 321 were of Japanese origin, 55 of English, 32 of American, 25 of German, and the rest mostly of Russian or French. In the 1960s, Feng Zikai (1898–1975) translated the *Genji monogatari* into Chinese. On the subject of books, it is interesting to note that the technique of modern bookbinding was also introduced from Japan to China at the end of the last century, when it replaced the traditional Chinese bookbinding system.

The May Fourth movement in 1919 was due largely to scholars and writers such as Lu Xun (1881–1936), Zhou Zuoren (1884–1967), Guo Moruo (1892–1978), Chen Duxiu (1880–1942), Li Dazhao (1889–1925) and Yu Dafu (1896–1944), who were educated at one time or another in Japan, and also to the new educational system and the books read by the students which, as we have seen, owed much to Japanese influence. Although at that time public opinion in Japan was in general unfavourable to the May Fourth movement, the scholar and political scientist Yoshino Sakuzō (1878–1933) did not hesitate to lend his support to the students of Peking University. Most of the pioneers of the May Fourth movement must have observed the remarkable result of the Meiji Restoration and the trend, discernible in daily usage, away from the literary towards the spoken style of the Japanese language.

Thus it was that Japan made a very real and important contribution to modernization and cultural reform in China. Between 1901 and 1939, some 12,000 Chinese students were educated in Japanese schools and colleges, and Japanese universities produced some 5,800 Chinese graduates. The largest number of university graduates – 1,787 – came from Meiji University, followed by Waseda University with 1,383. Keio University also played its part with 101, the relatively small number being explained, I think, by the smaller overall student intake and the policy and admission pattern of Keio University. And Keio can congratulate itself that the good influence of its education given many years ago is still making itself felt. For the Chinese writer Zhang Guangren (1902–), better known under the *nom de plume* Hu Feng, has recently come to prominence as the recipient of considerable attention among scholars of modern Chinese literature, both in Japan and in China. You may recall that he was criticized by Mao Zedong (1893–1976) in the early fifties. He was enrolled as a student in the English Department of Keio University between 1931 and 1933, although he left for family reasons without completing his studies.

Thus Japan, through her education system and particularly through her universities, became an agent of change in China. And here I link the past with the present and the future, for universities, if they deserve the name, must be agents of change.

This may seem to be a surprising statement: are not universities, you may ask, custodians of the cultural heritage and history of their nations, and as such do they not have a tendency, indeed a duty, towards tradition and conservation? It is certainly true that universities have an obligation to pass on to future generations the accumulated knowledge and wisdom of past generations. But it is also true that – to quote the memorable words of Franklin D. Roosevelt – 'we must reform if we would conserve'. Universities, their teachers and their students, should be no mere blind custodians of the relics of the past, tending an ancient shrine in which the flame of inspiration burns low. Hence the emphasis in universities on research as well as teaching, on pioneering new boundaries of knowledge, on pushing forward the creative frontiers of the mind. The past and its heritage is no mere boxed treasure. It must be laid open, sifted and critically appraised with new techniques and insights being brought to bear in its interpretation. Our students are not there just to receive; they are there to learn to think for themselves, to flex their minds, to exploit their own human resources. It is one of the roles of a university to be the conscience of society, to question the *status quo*. 'It is man's ability to say "No" which brings about progress.'

This is the paradox of a university. To the reactionary, it can appear to be a hotbed of revolution since it must be open to new ideas; to the revolutionary, it can be seen as an atrophied institution which resists change. It should, of course, be neither of these. In Paris in 1973, Professor J.D. Legge of Monash University addressed the International Association of Universities on the subject of the university's role in society and what he had to say then is worth quoting: 'The task of the universities,' he said, 'is to question firmly held assumptions, to challenge prejudice, to assist society in forming or changing its perception of itself, and to serve as sanctuaries where argument is open and where thought cannot be coerced except by argument. They are not "citadels of truth" ... but places where the question "What is truth?" is never finally answered.'

To be this and to do this, universities must have autonomy, the recognized right to make their own academic decisions. It is perhaps worth spending a few moments trying to define what we should, and what we should not, mean by 'autonomy' in this context. I do not, of course, wish to imply that I advocate total freedom for the academic to do as he wants and to spend public money as he fancies, though freedom of speech and the responsibility of spending, within one's budget, must be allowed. Perhaps the most helpful definition was one given in the form of categories at the General Conference of the International Association of Universities held in Tokyo in 1965. The conference identified four main categories or areas in which it considered freedom from outside control to be essential. These were: first, the selection of teachers and administrators; secondly, the selection of students; thirdly, the setting of the curricula to be followed in teaching and of the standards of attainment for the award of its degrees and qualifications; and fourthly, the choice of its research programmes.

All four of these freedoms need to be guarded with vigilance against encroachment from outside pressure or control. The most obvious would-be controller is usually the government, since universities increasingly rely on public finance made available to them through government machinery. The attempt at control may be undisguisedly political, as in the case of the South African government's veto on the admission of individual students; but more often the motives are benevolent, if misguided. Some governments seek to impose their own pattern on the universities which they finance, to make them reflect the values of society. They do not realize that, if they succeed, they would be merely providing an expensive form of either a high school or a technological institute, producing graduates who must be fitted into predetermined and narrowly based employment, without the flexibility of mind to diversify or innovate. The result may well be detrimental to the future of the nation for the sake of present expediency, for the outcome of such short-sightedness could be the reverse of what they expect. The graduates of a free university are agents of change, but they should also have acquired a sense of judgment and discernment, and have a debt of loyalty to the community which nurtured them.

But governments are not the only bodies outside the university which are potential sources of interference. The control over curricula leading to professional qualifications which certain professional societies often see fit to exert, using recognition as a weapon to exact acquiescence, could do considerable harm to university education. The aim of a university is surely not merely to impart technical expertise and know-how to its students, but also to develop their intellect and ability to think for themselves. Professional societies have a legitimate duty to safeguard the standards of and eligibility for their profession, but they should not be so single-minded in this pursuit that they work to diminish the higher and wider responsibility of the university.

It is perhaps surprising that even graduate associations, often with the best intentions, sometimes wield undue and unwholesome influence over the affairs of their Alma Mater. I know of at least one institution in the United States which, during its reorganization and upgrading, found resistance from its own graduates to be one of the worst obstacles against progress. Another university in Southeast Asia which I know well, had the dubious blessing of having an association of graduates some of whose members made it their regular business to oversee the running of the university, through political or any other means at their disposal, and contributed in large measure to the final downfall of their Alma Mater. In the University of Hong Kong, we have the good fortune of having graduates who leave us well alone in the running of our affairs, but who are never found lacking when help is needed. Some of our most generous benefactors are past students.

University autonomy is thus not a simple matter of freedom versus control, with regard to governments or to other pressure groups. Universities must be accountable; yet they must have the basic academic freedoms. The situation is complex, leading to searching questions and often fierce controversy. How does one reconcile the legitimate needs of government to obtain value for the taxpayers' money with the university's insistence on autonomy? Is the selection of students based entirely on academic merit, or is it influenced by consideration of race, creed or religion? On this I should state my own conviction that access to higher education is the natural and legitimate aspiration of the young: academic merit should therefore be the main, if not only, criterion. And what about the selection and promotion of teachers? Again, I can state my own view that political considerations should have no role in this: scholarship, experience and other appropriate academic qualities should, as far as I am concerned, be the only valid criteria. Other questions also come to mind, but although no less searching, they are less easy to decide using only principles as a guide. If universities cannot themselves keep their students in order, are they not forfeiting their right to autonomy? To what extent should a society's predictions for graduate manpower requirements determine or influence the university's curricula? What roles should professional associations be allowed in the setting of curricula, or graduate groups in university governance? As to research programmes, should these be as the academics fancy, or 'mission oriented' to solve immediate problems of the community? It is not easy to achieve the golden mean. All these, in fact, are questions on which each society and university must attempt to legislate for itself, to accommodate without abandoning principles, but there are no quick answers. In Hong Kong we have an organization based on the British system of an independent grants committee which, so to speak, stands between the universities and the government, the main source of finance. Its prototype in the United Kingdom has recently come in for severe criticism as this system obviously works much better in times of economic expansion than during retrenchment, and this should serve as a warning to us in Hong Kong that the ideal has perhaps not yet been attained.

Japanese universities have a great and inspiring tradition of freedom from outside interference and it is this which has enabled them to have such an influence for good both within and outside the borders of Japan. It is a tradition of autonomy envied by many of your counterparts in the region. If I might be allowed a personal recollection, I will mention the occasion of my first visit to Japan and what particularly impressed me then. It was in 1965 when, as head of the University of Malaya, I participated in the 4th General Conference of the International Association of Universities which was held in Tokyo, the first of four such conferences I have had the privilege of attending. One of the two themes of that conference was 'University autonomy – its meaning today'. There were some six hundred delegates from all over the world, and one of the places in Tokyo of particular historical interest that was shown to us was the *Enzetsukan*, or Hall of Public Speaking, in this very university. I was greatly impressed by the fact that, as long ago as the beginning of the Meiji period, a university had the vision and courage to create, in the *Enzetsukan*, such a place of intellectual debate where anyone was free to speak his mind without fear of repression. This is, indeed, a place of which all of you in Japan may well feel proud. It for me was an inspiring experience. That this tradition of freedom of speech and thought has continued to this day is an indication of the impact which Japanese universities have had on their nation and it is a good augury for the future.

It is, I think, no coincidence that Japan leads the world in modernization, for she has cultivated that freedom in her universities which has encouraged change in its most positive and creative sense. Years of progressive and liberal education have produced a graduate body which combines loyalty to the ideals and traditional virtues of Japan with the determination to exploit to the full for the nation's benefit all advances in scientific and technological knowledge. In this tradition Keio University, through its founder Fukuzawa Yukichi and those who subsequently inherited his legacy, takes its rightful place of pride and achievement.

References

Chen Qitian, *Jindai Zhongguo jiaoyushi* (Taipei: Taiwan Zhonghua Book Company, 1969)

Jansen, Marius B., *The Japanese and Sun Yat-sen* (California: Stanford University Press, 1979)

Luo Xianglin, *Xianggang yu Zhongxi wenhua zhi jiaoliu* (Hong Kong: Institute of Chinese Culture, 1961)

Sanetō Keishū, *Chūgokujin Nihon ryūgakushi*, enlarged edition (Tokyo: Kuroshio Shuppan, 1970)

—*Chūgokujin ryūgakusei shidan* (Tokyo: Daiichi Shobō, 1981).

Glossary

The following is a list of Chinese characters supplied to aid in the identification of the various people, societies, works and events mentioned in Dr Huang's paper.

Bairi Weixin   百日維新

Chen Duxiu   陳獨秀

Chen Qitian   陳啓天

Chūgokujin Nihon ryūgakushi   中國人日本留學史

Chūgokujin ryūgakusei shidan   中國人留學生史談

Dōbun Kai   同文會

Dong Biwu   董必武

Feng Zikai   豐子愷

Genji monogatari   源氏物語

Guantang jilin   觀堂集林

Guo Moruo   郭沫若

He Xiangning   何香凝

He Yingqin   何應欽

Huang, Rayson Lisung   黃麗松

Hu Feng   胡風

Hu Hanmin   胡漢民

Jiang Jieshi (Chiang Kai-shek)   蔣介石

Jiang Zuobin   蔣作賓

Jindai Zhongguo jiaoyushi   近代中國教育史

Kang Youwei   康有為

Liang Qichao   梁啓超

Liao Chengzhi   廖承志

Liao Zhongkai   廖仲愷

Li Dazhao   李大釗

Luo Xianglin   羅香林

Luo Xuetang xiansheng quanji   羅雪堂先生全集

Luo Zhenyu   羅振玉

Lu Xun   魯迅

Mao Zedong   毛澤東

Miyazaki Torazō   宮崎虎藏

Nakayama   中山

Ōkuma Shigenobu   大隈重信

Qiangxue Hui   強學會

Rong Hong (Yung Hung)   容閎

Sanetō Keishū   実藤惠秀

Sun Wen   孫文

Sun Yatsen   孫逸仙

Sun Zhongshan   孫中山

Wang Guantang xiansheng quanji   王觀堂先生全集

Wang Guowei   王國維

Wang Jingwei   汪精衛

Xianggang yu Zhongxi wenhua zhi jiaoliu

香港與中西文化之交流

Yan Xishan   閻錫山

Yoshino Sakuzō   吉野作造

Yu Dafu   郁達夫

Zeng Guofan   曾國藩

Zhang Guangren   張光人

Zhang Zhidong   張之洞

Zhongguo jindai chuban shiliao   中國近代出版史料

Zhou Enlai   周恩来

Zhou Zuoren   周作人

Whither Malaysia?

MAHATHIR BIN MOHAMAD

Change in human society is unavoidable. Much of this change is beyond control. But certain changes can be prevented or directed. Thus certain traditions and values may be consciously preserved while those changes which are permitted to take place can be set in a desired direction.

Malaysian society is one of those societies which has undergone and is undergoing rapid changes. Whereas prior to independence the changes were not properly regulated – and certainly they could not be directed by Malaysians – the period since independence in 1957 has seen numerous attempts to direct changes in order to maximize benefit for the Malaysian society and nation. The Malaysian development plans and the various policies, particularly the policy on education, were all direct attempts at ensuring that the changes that take place follow a predetermined course.

Certain years during the period of independence have been more remarkable in determining changes than others. Thus the launching of the Second Malaya Plan marked an attempt to bring the rural areas and its populace within the mainstream of the nation's development. Then came the riots of May 1969 and the soul-searching that followed. As a result, in 1970 the New Economic Policy (NEP) was born with the twin objectives of eradicating poverty, irrespective of race, and restructuring society so as to remove the identification of race with economic function.

Much has been done since the formulation of the NEP, which has had a profound effect on the changes in Malaysian society. Absolute poverty has never been a problem in Malaysia but relative poverty abounds. The NEP has achieved much to reduce relative poverty. Education and training have made vertical mobility an instrument for both poverty eradication and

150

restructuring. A variety of government schemes and institutions have improved the lot of the peasant farmers, petty traders, and the unskilled and semi-skilled workers. The *bumiputeras*, or indigenous people, have become more urbanized, have entered the mainstream of a modern monetized economy, and have gained access to the abundant wealth of the country. Equitableness has been largely achieved by a system of share-ownership pioneered by the biggest unit trust in the world, the National Equity Corporation (PNB). Any *bumiputera* who cares to save ten ringgit can own at least a hundred ringgit worth of shares in the huge plantation, mining, banking and trading companies in the country. The unit trust scheme was adopted in order that public/government-owned enterprises do not benefit only those *bumiputeras* who have money. A limit of 50,000 shares per person prevents domination of the trust by a few rich investors.

The NEP can be said to have changed the scene in Malaysia almost completely. No longer are the towns largely Chinese, and the kampongs populated mainly by Malays and other indigenous people; more and more, the urban areas are representative of the wide population structure of the nation.

Obviously not everything is satisfactory, nor are all the targets met. There is much to criticize. Some will say that the *bumiputeras* are still poor compared to the non-*bumiputeras*, while others will complain that the achievements so far have focused on material wealth. Like all criticisms they have elements of truth but, by any standard, the changes achieved have been remarkable. They are rendered even more remarkable because they have been achieved under stable conditions, in a democratic context. Certainly, few newly independent countries have achieved this much without resorting to totalitarian methods and traumatic upheavals.

The question now is whether the need is merely to implement the NEP or to do something more, so that not only will the twin aims be achieved, but the achievements themselves will become less reversible. In other words, the basic reasons or causes for the economic disparities between the races, and the inability of Malaysia until now to become a developed nation must be studied, understood, and – where necessary – corrected. Development plans *per se* do not result in development. Something more is needed. And it is that something more that the Malaysian government is after now. If that something is not to be found at home, then Malaysia must look abroad. And it is in searching for a foreign model that Malaysia decided that it must 'Look East'.

In the days when communication was poor, societies wishing to adopt foreign systems were able to be more selective. The people as a whole were not knowledgeable enough of conditions in other societies to be able to adopt values and systems of their own accord. With modern communication facilities, controlled and selective adoption of systems or values is less easy. The result is that in the developing countries values are absorbed which are in fact detrimental to them.

Thus there are some developing countries which have adopted wholesale some of the systems found in the advanced countries, such as the trade union system and philosophy. As they are developing countries and do not possess either the necessary infrastructure or vast resources and expertise, these countries are often placed at a disadvantage.

As the values and systems are adopted by the people without direction from the policy-makers, there is no way for them to be selective. The result of learning from foreign models can therefore be quite distressing.

Indeed, rapid communication has resulted in more of the deleterious values being adopted than the good ones. It follows that, left to themselves, the peoples of developing countries are more likely to subvert their own future than promote their well-being.

Governments of developing countries must therefore try as best they can to influence the selection of systems and values of the people. The most vociferous objections will, of course, come from the people of certain developed countries. They are likely to accuse such government leadership of denying freedom for the people. Basic to their attitude is their fear that, first, the developing countries may cease to be a market for the simple manufactured products that they like to dump; and secondly, that these countries might actually invade and compete with them in their own markets. Japan must be very familiar with this attitude. Resistance to Japanese penetration of the traditional markets of the old developed countries has never abated.

When the government of Malaysia decided to give some guidance to the people as to what they should copy, it was not too difficult for the choice to be made. The rags to riches story of Japan is well known and so is the story of South Korea. Malaysia may be said to be in the 'rags' stage that Japan found herself in during the years immediately after the Pacific War. Malaysia obviously cannot go through the slow evolution that characterized European development. The development must be rapid, indeed to a certain extent even more rapid than that of Japan.

When the Look East policy was adopted, although a careful study was made, it is possible that some areas were overlooked. Nevertheless it was realized that looking to Japan, for example, does not mean doing everything the Japanese way. Indeed it would be quite impossible to do so for a variety of reasons, among which is the lack of time available.

The most important thing that seems to have contributed to Japan's success is the work ethic. Some Japanese academics, and even journalists, may dispute the kind of perception of the Japanese work ethic that Malaysians have. But there can be little doubt that this work ethic differs greatly from those of the West, especially those of Britain and Australia.

The idea that something may be had for nothing is very much the basis of the present attitude towards work that is found in Western countries. Hence demands are made for better pay and benefits without relating these to productivity and better earnings for the establishment. In the days when empires were available as captive markets, such an attitude might not have been too harmful. But these days, no country has a captive market, nor does any country have a monopoly of the technologies of manufacturing. Consequently, increasing wages and benefits without a commensurate rise in productivity can only result in being priced out of the market. The fact is that nothing is free in this world or the next. Everything requires investment. In the words of a former Malaysian Minister of Finance, 'If you want something free then you must pay for it.' That payment may be in the form of hard work and greater productivity. If not, then economic decline will be the price.

Hence the Look East policy is initially and largely concerned

with learning and practising Japanese and Korean work ethics.
First, we want Malaysians to work as hard as the Japanese.
Lack of skill can be made up, at least partly, by a willingness to
work hard. It is well known that practice makes perfect. Working hard means more frequent practice. Eventually skill will be
acquired.

In business great value is attached to fulfilling undertakings.
If goods or services are promised for a certain date, it is important that this delivery date is kept. Working normal hours, or
worse still, working less than the normal hours will certainly
not help to meet delivery dates. Hence working hard means
achieving targets at no increase in cost, or even at lower cost. In
the West, work may be purposely delayed in order to create
some overtime work with double wages.

Working hard also does not mean shoddy or poor quality
work. The Japanese used to be known the world over for poor
quality. But today the story is totally different. Japanese products are known for their quality. Basically this is due to hard
work, a willingness to check and double-check every item
painstakingly in order to ensure the best quality.

The virtues of hard work are many. We believe that the
Japanese are imbued with these virtues. Even Japanese trade
unions are conscious of the need to work hard. Malaysians cannot be wrong if they conclude that the main reason for the
Japanese success story is the willingness to work hard. Malaysians cannot be derided if they wish to copy the Japanese work
ethic in the belief that they will be, if not equally successful, at
least better off than they are now.

The Japanese work ethic does not end with hard work, of
course. The democracy of the Japanese business organization is
quite unique. Differences in status between the executives and
the workers are not emphasized. They wear the same uniforms
and the executives tend to spend more time on the shop floor
than in their offices. When decisions are to be made everyone is
consulted. Even junior executives seem to have a say. It is not
only the board which decides. To a certain extent this slows
down decision-making, but it is probably compensated for by
the commitment of the personnel to the final decision when it is
made.

The cradle-to-grave type of relationship within Japanese

companies, at least the big ones, is another distinctive feature that Malaysians regard as worthy of study and possibly emulation. Large Japanese companies are paternalistic towards their employees. This is reciprocated by workers being more loyal to the companies.

We believe that the Japanese work ethic is not a traditional phenomenon. It represents a cultivated value system. Of course, traditional Japanese values play a role, an important role. But in the past the system was quite different. Thus, making quality almost a point of honour is an attitude which certainly did not exist prior to the Pacific War, when Japanese goods were synonymous with shoddiness.

Now, if it is the Japanese work ethic that has contributed to the economic and commercial success of post-war Japan, and if this work ethic could be acquired and developed artificially, it follows that Malaysians too can shape and develop their own work ethic. This is precisely what the Look East policy is all about.

But, of course, there are other aspects of the Japanese economic miracle that are worthy of study and possible emulation. Although Malaysia is rich in resources and endowed with considerable tracts of land suitable for the cultivation of a variety of profitable agricultural produce, there is no reason why there should not be manufacturing industries. How Japan introduced manufacturing and developed it until it could compete with the industrial West is also worthy of study and emulation.

Then there are the highly successful Japanese marketing strategies. It is claimed that the *sōgō-shōsha* (general trading companies) are not profitable, but there is no doubt that in the early days it was the *sōgō-shōsha* which opened up trade on a large scale and promoted Japanese goods. How they did this is again worthy of study and emulation.

One of the accusations made by competing Western companies is that Japanese companies seem to be indistinguishable from the Japanese government. They felt that they were up against the whole Japanese nation when competing with Japanese companies. Hence, the coining of the term 'Japan Incorporated', meaning the whole of the Japanese nation seems to be incorporated into one company, which then challenges the individualistic and mutually competing industries of the West. Of course, this is not completely true. Japanese companies do compete with each other when marketing goods or bidding for contracts. Indeed, Japanese companies have joined hands with non-Japanese companies to compete against other Japanese companies. But, by and large, the Japanese companies are backed by the Japanese government and workers whenever they compete with non-Japanese companies abroad. At home, a large degree of protection is afforded to Japanese companies, which makes it extremely difficult for foreign manufacturers to penetrate Japanese markets. The impression that there is a Japan Incorporated is thus quite justified.

But to Malaysia, which is quite incapable of competing with the Japanese in any case, the concept of Japan Incorporated is interesting as a device for the development of the Malaysian economy. Historically, the government regarded itself as the opponent of the private sector. It sees privately owned companies as avaricious and prone to all sorts of extra-legal activities at the expense of the government, the people and the country. There is some justification for this. The fact that in the past most businesses in Malaysia were individually owned and antagonistic towards government policies merely reinforces the antagonism of government officials.

Even when the government understood the need, and did give protection to Malaysian industries, this was done with reluctance and a great deal of suspicion. Officials adopt a most intrusive attitude towards the private sector at all times. Clearly no one could appreciate that the national interest is what suffers when businesses are unduly obstructed by government red tape.

On the other hand, the private sector too felt antagonistic towards the government and government officials in particular. The private sector assumed that the government was out to frustrate them, to obstruct businesses and to make enterprises unprofitable. Officials, as agents of the government, were regarded with veiled hostility. The only time when the businessman seemed friendly was when he wished to buy an official. Otherwise the relationship was one of unconcealed confrontation.

The private sector consequently takes a dim view of all

government policies. No matter what the reasons are, government policies are regarded as an unnecessary imposition calculated to make life more difficult for the business community. The genuineness of the government's efforts to create an atmosphere conducive to stability, which must benefit business as a whole, is questioned or rejected offhand.

Needless to say, the officiousness of officials and the distrust of government and officials by the business community do not contribute towards the kind of economic growth that a developing country like Malaysia needs. To lubricate and stimulate that growth, both the public and private sectors must contribute and co-operate in facilitating economic activity.

In Malaysia there is an additional problem. Unlike Japan, Malaysia is multiracial. Worse still, the different races are not equally developed economically. Thus the Malays are largely peasant farmers in the rural areas, the Indians work and live on large rubber estates, while the Chinese are traders and entrepreneurs living in urbanized communities.

It is well known that class disparity often leads to serious confrontation. Indeed, it is class division that gave rise to communist and socialist ideologies and the bloody revolutions in many European and eastern countries. But when, in addition to class differences, you have a complementary and reinforcing racial difference, then the potential for conflicts and clashes is even greater. And, of course, differences and class-cum-racial tensions do not contribute to a smooth economic growth.

In the case of Malaysia, the first step that was taken was to eliminate the identification of race with economic function. This means that conscious efforts have to be made to ensure that all occupations at all levels have proportionate racial representation. In other words, there should be as many Malays and Indians in the urban centres as there are Chinese. The races must be thoroughly and evenly mixed. Economic prosperity, in particular, should not be confined to one race only.

The New Economic Policy's 20-year Perspective Plan which was launched in 1970 has this objective. In the thirteen years that this plan has been implemented a fair degree of success has been achieved. Today Malaysian towns and cities no longer look like exclusively Chinese towns. There are large and efficient companies run by the indigenous people, the *bumiputeras*, or 'sons of the soil'. There are also a number of large funds that belong to *bumiputeras* which can be invested so that the *bumiputera* share of equity is maintained. In addition, the federal and state governments have set up a number of corporations to represent *bumiputeras* in various enterprises.

Consequently, the private sector is now more representative of the different communities than before. The 'Malaysia Incorporated' concept, whereby the government helps the private sector, would therefore benefit not only the Chinese who previously controlled that sector but all the communities. If the Malaysia Incorporated concept and privatization were not acceptable before, it was partly because they would only increase the disparities between the races that had been a feature of Malaysia in the past. Nevertheless, as the restructuring of the economic configuration in Malaysia is not yet completed, the government will have to be very vigilant that the Malaysia Incorporated concept and privatization do not stir up racial tensions.

The Look East policy and the desire to copy from Japan is clearly not a blank cheque. Malaysia wants to learn from Japan but has to be selective. The socio-political and cultural differences between Japan and Malaysia must always be borne in mind. Economic growth and development are not the sole determinants. More important than anything else is the racial harmony and political stability of the country.

We in Malaysia believe that we have succeeded better than anyone else in achieving racial harmony, or at least in reducing racial antagonism to manageable levels. Since independence in 1957 we have had only one major racial clash, and that was controlled within a period of just over a year. Since then, stability has been palpable. Malaysia has in fact developed at a much more rapid pace after the riots of 1969 than before. This is not to say that the riots were necessary. But it does demonstrate to all the races in Malaysia the folly of allowing narrow racialism to take over. Since the riots, pragmatism has largely won the day. Everyone has learned that in Malaysia no single race can have all that it wants for itself.

Indeed, Malaysia can be regarded as doing well only when everyone, every race, is fairly unhappy. Should one particular racial group be very satisfied and happy, it could only mean that their wishes have been catered for at the expense of the other races. If this should happen, sooner or later there are bound to be racial clashes, political instability and economic disruption.

It is because of this need to balance the well-being of the different races in Malaysia, and to prevent confrontation and racial disturbances, that policies for Malaysia's development must be carefully formulated and implemented. The timing of these policies is also extremely crucial.

The Look East, Malaysia Incorporated, and privatization policies and concepts could not have been introduced earlier. They would have been almost entirely unacceptable to the deprived indigenous people. But even now these policies must be prudently implemented. Foreigners must appreciate that they are dealing with a sensitive multiracial society. If they are required to conform to certain non-economic requirements in their economic involvement in Malaysia, it is really for their own good. The economy of the nation, any nation, cannot prosper as long as there are civil and political upheavals.

There is a price to be paid for everything. In the case of Malaysia, the price of stability is a somewhat slower economic development. In the final analysis, however, this is a small price to pay.

Hence changes in Malaysia must be carefully planned and timed. It is not a matter of issuing an edict; rather, it is one of cautious introduction and clarification of policies and their implementation. But, God willing, in the end the target will be achieved.

These are the changes that are taking place in Malaysia. They are not quite spontaneous. They are the result of fairly carefully thought-out planning. Probably they are not perfect. But then no planning is absolutely perfect. They will have to be corrected as we go along. But it is important that everyone, including foreigners, understand and are guided by them. Then, and only then, can a degree of success be achieved.

Notes on Contributors

Ishikawa Tadao
President of Keio University, Japan; Professor, Department of Political Science. Professor Ishikawa's other posts include: Director, Japanese Association of International Relations; Director, Asian Pacific Association of Japan; President, Private Universities Association of Japan; President, University Chartering Council, Ministry of Education; Director, International Association of Universities; member, Trilateral Commission of Japan, USA and Europe. Publications include *A Study of the History of the Communist Party in China* (1959); *International Politics and Mainland China* (1968); *Problems of Contemporary China* (1969); *Japanese Diplomacy in my Eyes* (1976).

Park Choong Hoon
Chairman, Korea Industrial Development Institute; member, Advisory Council on State Affairs. Honours: Honorary LLD from Illinois Wesleyan University, USA. Past appointments include: Acting Prime Minister and Acting President of the Republic of Korea (1980); President and Chairman of the Korean Traders Association (1973); Deputy Prime Minister and Minister of Economic Planning (1967); Minister of Commerce and Industry (1963); Director, Foreign Trade Bureau (1948).

Mr Park is a graduate of Doshisha College of Commerce, Japan.

Mochtar Lubis
Director General, Press Foundation of Asia (Manila); Associate Editor, Wordpaper (Boston). Mr Lubis played an active part in the independence movement in Indonesia, later turning to journalism and writing. His interests are wide-ranging, covering

politics, economics, literature and ecology. Awards include two from the BMKN (Indonesian National Cultural Congress), Indonesian National Book Award, Magsaysay Award, Golden Pen Award of the International Association of Publishers and Editors, Presidential Award for the Arts. Publications include *Jalan Tak Ada Ujung* (The Road with no End) on the Indonesian fight for freedom; *Catatan Korea* (Korean Notes) on the Korean War; *Indonesia Today*.

Suzuki Takao

Professor, Institute for Linguistic and Cultural Studies, Keio University, Japan; Chairman, Graduate School of Human Relations, Keio University. Past appointments include: member of the Council for National Language (1975–81); Visiting Fellow, Downing College, Cambridge University (1980); Visiting Fellow, Emmanuel College, Cambridge University (1979); Visiting Professor, Yale University (1977); Visiting Fellow, Australian National University (1975); Visiting Professor, University of Illinois (1971). Publications include *Language and Culture* (1972); *A Closed Language, the World of Japanese* (1975); *An Inquiry into Language as a Study of Man* (1978).

Sommai Hoontrakool

Minister of Finance, Thailand; President, Thai-Japanese Association. Honours: Knight Grand Cordon (Special Class) of the Most Exalted Order of the White Elephant; Knight Grand Cross (First Class) of the Most Illustrious Order of Chula Chom Klao; First Class of the Order of the Sacred Treasure of Japan; Honorary Doctor of Economics, Keio University, Japan. With a background in banking, Mr Sommai has been three times appointed Minister of Finance.

He is a graduate of Keio University, and has played an active role in furthering Thai-Japanese relations.

Escolastica B. Bince

Consultant, Central Bank of the Philippines, Republic of the Philippines. After working as an Assistant at the University of the Philippines, in 1941 Mrs Bince was appointed to the National Enterprise Control Board. In 1949 she joined the newly founded Central Bank of the Philippines and went on to serve as Special Assistant to the Governor and later as Deputy Governor. Since retiring in 1982 she has served as a consultant to the Bank.

Sun Shangqing

Deputy Secretary-General, Chinese Academy of Social Sciences, People's Republic of China. Professor Sun's other posts include: Standing Secretary-General, Center for Technology and Economic Studies, State Council; Professor, Economics Department of Beijing University; Vice-President, Chinese Society for Production Economics; Vice-Chairman, Executive Council, Chinese Association of Industrial Management. Publications include *Economy and Management* (1981); *Chinese Industrial Structures* (1981); *A New Road for the Chinese Economy* (1982); *The Advancing Chinese Economy* (1983); *On the Strategy for Economic Structures* (1984).

Albert Wendt

Professor of Pacific Literature, University of the South Pacific, Western Samoa. Professor Wendt is a graduate of Victoria University, New Zealand. As both a writer and an academic, his novels, poems and articles have been published in many foreign languages. Novels: *Sons for the Return Home*; *Pouliuli*; *Leaves of the Banyan Tree*; short stories: *Flyingfox in a Freedom Tree*; poems: *Inside Us the Dead*.

Rayson Lisung Huang

Vice-Chancellor, University of Hong Kong. Honours: Honorary DSc from the University of Hong Kong. Dr Huang's past appointments include: Vice-Chancellor, Nanyang University (1969); Chair of Chemistry, University of Malaya in Kuala Lumpur (1959). Honorary posts include: Fellow Member, World Academy of Arts and Sciences (FWA); President, Association of Southeast Asian Institutions of Higher Learning

(ASAIHL); Chairman of Council, Association of Commonwealth Universities (ACU); unofficial member, Legislative
Council, Hong Kong.

Dr Huang has received a DPhil and DSc from Oxford University, and a DSc from the University of Malaya.

Mahathir bin Mohamad
Prime Minister and Minister of Defence, Malaysia. Dr
Mahathir first became active in politics in 1945; he has been a
member of the Kedah Malay Union, Saberkas, and the Kedah
Malay Youth Movement. He is the President of the United Malays
National Organization, the leading partner in the National
Front, the ruling party. Originally a medical officer, he was
elected to parliament in 1964 and appointed Minister of Education in 1974. After occupying various cabinet positions, in 1981
he became the fourth Prime Minister of Malaysia. In 1970 he
published *The Malay Dilemma*.

Index

agreed specialization, 24
agriculture, 69–70, 98. *See also* rice
arms race, 18, 39, 43, 44, 46, 49–50
Asia: awareness of crisis, 9, 10; difficulty in defining, 8–9; historical consciousness, 9; meeting with the West, 9–10, 56–7; perceptions of, 10; self-definition, 10; solidarity, 63
Asian Development Bank, 32
Asia–Pacific region: need for co-operative framework, 21, 23–5; need to rediscover identity, 17; obstacles to co-operation, 22, 24, 25; potential, 17, 19–20; regional culture, 26; security, 18; tasks, 16–17
Asquith (prime minister of England), 67
Axis, Berlin–Tokyo, 34

Baoshan (steel works), 55
bookbinding, 140–41
Britain, 35, 70–1, 76, 123–4, 145
Buddhism, 68
bumiputera, 151, 157–8
Bunmei Kaika, 1

capitalism, 29, 32, 43, 73
CAPTAIN system, 38
Central Bank of the Philippines: charter, 81, 89; supervision of OBUs, 85; debt management, 96; interest rate policy, 91–3; open market operations, 90–91; promotional activities, 96–7; rediscount operations, 89–90; reforms, 86–9; role of, 81–2, 87; stabilization of the peso, 93–6
China: boilers, 106; changing technology structure, 113–14; coal processing, 109–10; coal reserves, 101, 102; education, 112, 140; elastic energy coefficient (ECE), 107–8; electricity output, 108–9; employment, 114–17; energy consumption, 106–7; hydro-electricity, 101–3; Japanese perceptions of, 59–60; oil reserves, 102, 103; relationship with Japan, 55, 100–1, 117–19, 136–8 *passim*; vehicle manufacture, 105–6
Chulalongkorn, King (of Thailand), 68, 78–9
Chun Doo Hwan (president of South Korea), 23–4
colonialism, 6, 57, 69, 70–71,